RICHARD CAME

SILVER

OCTOPUS BOOKS

Acknowledgments

Figure 106 is reproduced by gracious permission of Her Majesty the Queen; figures 9, 24, 44, 63, 73, 85, 101, 106 by courtesy of the Worshipful Company of Goldsmiths and figure 7 by courtesy of New College, Oxford.

Figure 111 appears by courtesy of the Museum of Fine Arts, Boston; figure 15 by permission of C. R. Love, Jr. and figure 88 by permission of the Philadelphia Museum of Art.

Figures 8, 11 appear by courtesy of the Art Institute of Chicago; figure 61 by permission of the Worcester Art Museum, Massachusetts; figures 71, 86 are reproduced by courtesy of Yale University Art Gallery (from the Mabel Brady Garvan Collection) and figure 69 by courtesy of the Henry Francis du Pont Winterthur Collection. Figure 26 is reproduced by courtesy of the Detroit Institute of Arts (from the Elizabeth Parke Firestone Collection of Early French Silver) and figures 108, 112, 119 by courtesy of the Metropolitan Museum of Art (from purchases made in 1933 from the Joseph Pulitzer Bequest, and from the Bequest of Catherine D. Wentworth, 1948). Figures 18, 25, 37, 54, 62, 65, 83, 103, 105, 114, 116 are reproduced by kind permission of Messrs S. J. Phillips, London.

Figures 7, 9, 14, 46, 63, 73, 91, 101, 106 are reproduced from the colour filmstrips produced for the Worshipful Company of Goldsmiths by Diana Wyllie Ltd; the photographs are by P. Delius, F.I.B.P., F.R.P.S. Figures 13, 17, 120 are by Photographie Giraudon; figure is by Raymond Fortt and figures 3–5, 22 are from the Mansell Collection.

Figures 19, 23, 30, 35, 41, 46, 50, 52, 55, 58, 78, 80, 84, 85, 91, 110 were photographed specially by Messrs A. C. Coopers, London, from the collection at the Victoria and Albert Museum, through the kindness of Mr C. C. Oman and the Department of Metalwork. Figures 26, 32, 51, 57, 60, 99 were taken by Messrs Coopers by courtesy of Messrs Christie, Manson and Woods; figures 74, 90, 97, 117 and all other photographs by courtesy of Messrs Sotheby, from pieces which have passed through both their rooms.

This edition first published 1972 by
OCTOPUS BOOKS LIMITED
59 Grosvenor Street, London W.1

ISBN   7064 0039 9

PRODUCED BY MANDARIN PUBLISHERS LIMITED AND PRINTED IN HONG KONG

Preceding page
A tea service by Paul Revere of Boston (1735–1815)

Goldsmiths and Marks
Techniques

1 An Elizabeth I Tigerware jug with silver-gilt mounts, 1567

THE COLLECTOR OR STUDENT of goldsmiths' work (using this term throughout to embrace workers in both gold and silver) should ideally be something of a historian. No other branch of the arts has been as subject as the goldsmiths' to wars, crises, fluctuations in trade or changes in taste. It was not until the middle of the nineteenth century that the conception of preserving earlier pieces purely on account of their age or artistic merit became generally accepted: until then gold and silver plate was regarded

3

2 The Arlington *Tazza*, a Henry VIII piece, London, 1532

3 Etienne Delaulne's engraving of his own workshop. He was a famous Parisian goldsmith of the sixteenth century

by its owner as a reserve to be consigned to the melting pot and converted to coin whenever the need arose. In this way gold and silver suffer a disadvantage encountered in no other branch of the applied arts; a picture, a piece of porcelain or furniture, reduced to its essentials, is quite valueless. There are innumerable cases of fine pieces of silver being melted shortly after they were made, particularly in seventeenth and eighteenth-century France. The continent of Europe, ravaged by wars, has lost far more in relation to its size than seabound Great Britain, with only the Civil War of 1642-1649 to disturb four centuries of relatively stable internal conditions and rising prosperity. In addition, records show that domestic silver in daily use received such hard wear that much of it had to be refashioned frequently, and when one considers that in great households silver took the places that china and porcelain occupy today, this is quite understandable. It

4 A goldsmith's shop in the fifteenth century; a miniature ascribed to Alexander Bening, the renowned Flemish illuminator, who died at Ghent in 1519.

is perhaps remarkable not that so much has disappeared but that so much has survived.

The beauty and artistry of many pieces cannot be fully appreciated unless something is understood of goldsmiths' techniques. Both gold and silver in their natural form are too soft for practical use, hence the necessity for alloying with another metal, normally copper, to give additional strength. This question of alloy is the basis of almost every early ordinance concerning or emanating from the goldsmiths' guilds, dealt with in greater detail below. After smelting, the molten metal, alloyed in accordance with the standards laid down by the guild concerned, was poured into moulds corresponding as far as possible to the shape of the object to be made. At this point the goldsmith's work begins; the basic tool of his craft for thousands of years has been the hammer. In past centuries distinctions between so-called hammermen of all kinds were less clear, and in some countries, particularly in the smaller centres, guilds of hammermen existed composed of blacksmiths, whitesmiths (or silversmiths), coppersmiths and others. The hammers used are extremely diverse, ranging in the past from the large forge hammers, used to beat out the ingot, to the long narrow examples used to raise a piece of silver. The hammers have a variety of faces, square, oblong and circular and in varying degrees of convexity. Wooden mallets, sometimes covered with hide, are also used.

Today silver sheet is supplied in any size required, obviating much preparatory work: in past centuries this was not so. The goldsmith, confronted with a cast plate, hammered it to the required thickness and size. If a coffee pot, a bowl, a jug or some similar object was being made, processes known as 'sinking', followed by 'raising' were employed. The silver sheet was first laid on a slightly hollowed wooden block or sandbag and hammered from the top until the shape of a shallow bowl had been achieved. The raising process which then followed, involved the use of a 'stake', if fixed, or a 'head', if detachable, which are varieties of small anvils in many sizes. Resting his piece on this, the goldsmith, using his many hammers at a high rate of accurate striking, hammered it into the shape required. As silver and gold become brittle and unworkable without the application of heat, the piece is heated constantly to approximately a dull red six hundred degrees centigrade, a process known as annealing. It is not usually realized that many old pieces raised by this process have no seam or junction of any kind whatsoever. To raise a narrow-necked jug from a flat sheet of metal, which may involve 'doming' (or hammering from the inner as well as from the outer side), requires considerable technical skill and a very accurate eye. Another method, which does involve a seam, was generally encountered with straight-sided examples, tapered cylindrical coffee pots, tankards or similar pieces. These were hammered and curved from the sheet and soldered generally along the line of the handle sockets where the join is virtually undetectable. For salvers, waiters and other pieces of plate, flat hammering was employed, which is an extremely skilled process; it is not as simple as it may appear to achieve an absolutely smooth, rigid surface.

5 Front and back views of a clasp made for Clement VII by Cellini, from a drawing by Bartoli

Essentially completed, the piece then had its additions soldered to it, handles, finials, salver feet and borders, lips to jugs etc. The additions and embellishments were almost invariably cast, although some handles were hammered up and soldered together. The only other instances where castings were used was in the manufacture of candlesticks, which were usually cast in two halves and soldered together, and plaques or reliefs (although even the latter were by no means always cast). The process of soldering requires great care, as the soldering metal has a melting point only slightly lower than that of silver.

Although there have been periods when predominantly plain silver has been fashionable, as a rule the surface of a piece is relieved by some form of decoration, even if this is only a monogram or coat of arms. The three principal ways of decorating a plain surface are embossing (or *repoussé* work), chasing and engraving. Embossing involves raising the surface of the metal in low relief, the process being carried out from the reverse in the case of a salver or tray, or from the inside where a jug or similar piece is being worked. To avoid distortion, the piece of silver is firmly bedded in or filled with pitch. Embossing a narrow-necked piece which cannot be punched from the inside is done by the use of a 'snarling-iron', which is a steel rod with an angled bend, the shorter arm ending in a knob, the longer being secured in a vice. Hammering near the fixed end causes the end of the rod to 'chatter' or vibrate on the inside of the piece and the appropriate raised design can thus be achieved. Merely a roughly raised pattern at this stage, it is then finished from the reverse or outside with small punches and a light hammer.

Chasing in general can be distinguished from engraving, in that the design can be seen on the reverse or inside of the pieces. Having outlined the pattern on the surface, the chaser cuts and at the same time slightly depresses the surface. A light hammer can be used in this process also, and to avoid distortion, the piece may be bedded in pitch. Finally, engraving involves the use of a tool made of tempered steel with a very sharp cutting point, known as a 'scorper'. The surface of the metal is scored by the engraver, and some of the meticulous engraving of past centuries repays close study under a glass: the minute attention to detail and the intricate work which go to make up a complex design are remarkable. An engraving process which was most widely used in England from about 1775

6 An Elizabeth I silver-gilt *tazza*, height 6 ins, 1599

to 1795 was 'bright-cut' work, in which the surface of the metal was actually cut away to give reflections on tiny facets, an attractive and highly skilled technique. The decorative processes described were generally specialised trades, although there have been goldsmiths capable of carrying out every stage of the work, from the cast plate to the chased and engraved final product.

After completion the piece was immersed in a weakened solution of sulphuric acid or 'pickle' and was then scoured perfectly clean. The maker then 'planished' a raised piece, hammering it evenly with a flat hammer polished to a mirror surface. Finally, in the past, it was turned over to women for the final polishing process, the only task traditionally performed by them. Burnishing by hand has been discontinued for probably a hundred years and all polishing is now done by machine.

Unfortunately manufacturing techniques have altered, for today the old processes are prohibitively expensive, taking eight or ten times as long as a machine. Commissions are inadequate to keep more than a bare handful of craftsmen working in the traditional way. A piece of modern silver which is made by the old methods still has a more pleasing surface, colour and texture than a factory-made piece and is often stronger.

While considering goldsmiths' techniques it is important to mention decoration added at a later date or restoration of such pieces. During the nineteenth century the vogue for ornate, profusely-embossed silver led to much inherited plate being sent to be embossed in the prevailing fashion. As a result one encounters what was once a well-proportioned and plain piece of silver utterly spoiled by over heavy work, its beauty ruined and its value considerably reduced. It surprises many that it is possible to emboss an earlier piece of silver, but as the technique involves no actual alteration in form it is not difficult. The tendency in this century has been to restore such pieces to their original condition, although the cost of this work is so high that unless on a potentially quite outstanding piece it is rarely carried out today. An old piece of silver acquires a patina which only years of use and care can give: examined under a glass the skin will be seen to have numerous small scratches and pitting, which combine in a perfect specimen to give a delightful feel, colour and appearance. Naturally,

7 An English silver-gilt hour-glass salt, *c.* 1490, from New College, Oxford

8 (*right*) A German ewer by Franz Dotte, Nuremberg, *c.* 1590

9 The Bowes Cup, a standing cup and cover of silver-gilt and rock-crystal, London, 1554

10 A Charles II ewer by Charles Shelley, London, 1666

11 An American Caudle cup by Cornelius Vanderburgh (1652–1699), New York, c. 1683

if a piece has been restored, this old patina is lost, and where such work has been badly done marks may be affected and a shiny, poor surface can result, because of the fresh hammering and annealing which is involved. Another case where surfaces may be affected is when an inscription or coat of arms has been removed. Family silver has often had engraved armorials, presentation inscriptions or initials, and on changing hands these were frequently removed, and replaced by others. Except in pieces of exceptionally heavy gauge, this usually results in some thinness of the metal, and it pays when examining a piece of silver to test its body by gentle pressure between finger and thumb. On occasions when engraving has been removed it has sometimes been necessary to insert a patch often disguised by decorative engraving. When a piece of silver is tarnished the solder lines show more clearly; in the same way patches or repairs may be distinguished by breathing on the surface. Another way of concealing repair work or adding body is electro-plating, ethically unpardonable but occasionally encountered. The colour and greasy surface should suffice to give this away. One also encounters cases where lips have been added to tankards to make jugs, feet have been replaced on salvers, plates and dishes have been re-shaped and similar alterations have been made. These were never intended to deceive but were merely private requirements carried out to bring pieces in line with contemporary taste. Unless the additions are hall-marked, however, these pieces cannot legally be sold, in England at least, at the present time. Fakes as such do exist, but as a rule some discrepancy in style, poor design and decoration, or worn marks where no wear would be expected, give them away. Today at least the collector has the advantage of advice from innumerable experts on the subject, an advantage his predecessor a century ago was largely forced to do without, but generalisations about faking are impossibile as individual examples differ to such a degree.

After a piece has passed visual inspection, the next step is to look at the hall-marks. The whole subject of marks is linked with the development of the goldsmiths' guilds and it is not generally realised how old these are. Most of the principal towns throughout Europe had well-established bodies of goldsmiths by the fourteenth century, and in all the large centres some mention of a town mark occurs by that period. The date-letter system,

12 One of a set of four German silver-gilt table candlesticks, Cologne, c. 1690

13 A design by Nicolas de Launay for pieces of silver executed for Louis XIV and the Duc d'Aumont, c. 1700

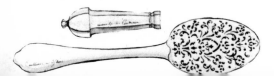

familiar particularly to French and English collectors, is of considerable antiquity. This system was not designed (as is so often thought) specifically to date a piece of silver: there would have been no object in this at a time when the antiquity of a piece was held of no account. It was merely a means of ascertaining which assay master was holding office, so that if a piece was found to be sub-standard after marking, both he and the maker could be held responsible.

The credit for first instituting an alphabetical system of dating goes to Montpellier in 1427, a necessary inno-vation as the town had the reputation in the previous century of producing the worst silver in the entire country. These varying standards had the effect of causing unscru-pulous goldsmiths to stamp low-quality work with the mark of another town, and as early as 1275 an ordinance reminding the guilds that each town should have its own mark was issued. In 1260 mention is made of the gold-smiths, in common with other Paris guilds, as being long established. In 1355 we have the first reference in Paris to a maker's mark, a device in use at the time; after 1540 initials were added also. Although the date-letter system did not become obligatory throughout France until 1506, it was almost certainly instituted in Paris at least fifty years before. Although taxes on gold and silver had been collected earlier from time to time, in 1672 a permanent system of taxation was begun, involving a so-called charge mark, struck when the piece was submitted in the rough for assay, marked with the date-letter and maker's mark in addition, and a discharge mark, struck on the finished piece after duty had been paid. These marks, namely a maker's mark, a date-letter, charge and discharge marks, remained in use until the Revolution when the marks changed completely. The guilds, which until then had been responsible through their wardens for assaying, marking and breaking sub-standard wares, with disciplinary and punitive powers, were finally dissolved in 1797. Since then it has remained the responsibility of the state. The marks introduced made it impossible to ascribe a piece to any one year, and after 1838 a single mark was used, which is still in existence.

The London marks are of particular interest, in that they have remained virtually unchanged from their intro-duction in the fifteenth century until the present day, a tradition which seems likely to continue in the future. In

11

14 A Henry VIII parcel-gilt hour-glass salt, 1516, the property of the Worshipful Company of Goldsmiths

15 An Elizabeth I parcel-gilt sideboard ewer and dish, London, 1567. The ewer is engraved around the rim with pictures of the Kings of England and within with scenes from the life of Joseph; now in the Collection of C. Ruxton Love, Jnr.

16 (*left and opposite*) A pair of Louis XV table candlesticks, Paris, 1735

17 Designs by Nicolas de Launay for pieces of silver for the King, *c.* 1700

the year 1180 an association of goldsmiths was fined for being irregularly established and in 1238 laws were introduced, setting standards for silver and gold and appointing six wardens to supervise the craft, as they did in Paris. The leopard's head, the famous London mark, is first mentioned as obligatory in 1300, although it was almost certainly in use over a century earlier. The London goldsmiths at this period were a numerous, wealthy and powerful body, and they were incorporated in 1327. In 1363 every master goldsmith was required to have his mark. The final and most important charter in 1462 gave them far-reaching powers not only in London but throughout the country, involving assay, the breaking of substandard silver, punishment of offenders, and other disciplinary powers. Recent research leads one to believe that a system of date-letters incorporated in the leopard's head was instituted at this time, a regular date-letter system in twenty-year cycles beginning in 1478. As in France, goldsmiths used symbols until about the middle of the sixteenth century, when initials began to be used. In 1543 the lion passant was added. From then onwards one finds the same four marks on London silver, a maker's mark, the lion passant, date-letter and leopard's head. Another series of marks with a somewhat higher silver standard (which can still be used) was introduced from 1697 to 1720. In addition, the reigning sovereign's head, which was a duty mark, appears from 1784 to 1890.

The guilds in Italy may well be the oldest of all: references are made to associations of goldsmiths in the tenth century. Roman statutes between 1358 and 1398 set standards for gold and silver, the latter conforming approximately to English sterling with the mark SP, or SPR if of a higher standard. Not until 1508 was a goldsmiths' guild as such incorporated, composed of secular smiths and others from the papal court. Four 'consuls' were appointed to superintend the trade, with the same powers that we have encountered elsewhere. Each goldsmith was expected to register a workshop mark, and a slightly lower silver standard and a higher gold standard were introduced. The marks SPQR, ROMA and the two keys appear for the first time. A personal mark was required in 1563 as well as the Rome stamp, the consul's countermark. In 1608 the famous umbrella and crossed keys appeared for the first time and continued to be used until 1811, when a radical change occured as a result of the annexation of the papal states by Napoleon two years earlier, and the marks conformed approximately to the French. Dates were stamped in the last half of the seventeenth century on Roman silver but this practice ceased or became erratic after about 1720. The goldsmiths of Rome were always somewhat indisciplined, probably as a result of the privileged position enjoyed by those working for the Papal Court, and the guild there never exercised the authority one encounters elsewhere. As a result a large amount of unmarked or inadequately marked Italian silver is to be found.

Germany, as might be expected with its multifarious guilds, had powerful goldsmiths' guilds by the fourteenth century. Mention is made in the thirteenth century of makers' marks, which, as elsewhere until the middle of the sixteenth century, tended to be devices, later giving place to initials. Both Nuremberg and Augsburg in the fourteenth century had regulations governing their goldsmiths, with set standards, supervisory and punitive powers. The famous Nuremberg mark, the letter N, came

18 A German toilet service made by Michael Hueter and Michael Hackel in Augsburg, c. 1710

19 A French casket in silver-gilt with crystal panels, c. 1560. Crystal was thought to detect the presence of poison

into regular use in 1516 and the equally well-known Augsburg mark, the pineapple, in 1529. In Nuremberg a date-letter system was only introduced in 1766, continuing somewhat erratically until the middle of the nineteenth century. Augsburg varied its pineapple mark with successive wardens until in 1735 a date-letter was introduced, falling into disuse at about the same time as in Nuremberg.

These principal centres of the goldsmithing industry have been mentioned as being of especial interest, but in other countries, notably the Netherlands and Scandinavia, highly organised guilds with similar systems of supervision existed. It is remarkable that such a consistently high standard (in most countries of approximately the same level) was, and in some cases still is, maintained for so many centuries, and this is largely due to the emphasis placed on marks.

The Influence of the Renaissance

20 A porcelain cup and cover, mounted in gold and enamels, attributed to Cellini

IT IS AN OLD TRUISM that the arts flourish in times of peace and wither in war, and this is particularly applicable to goldsmiths' work where, in the past, conditions of stability and free circulation of coin were vitally essential. France, in the medieval period the undisputed centre of the craft, had completely lost this ascendancy by 1500, which I have taken as a convenient starting point. The constant, crippling wars with England, as well as the domestic dissensions of Charles VIII's reign, were scarcely conducive

17

to a flourishing goldsmiths' trade and led to a mass migration of craftsmen to Flanders, where they settled in Bruges, Brussels and Ghent. The Wars of the Roses from 1455-1488 in England equally did not encourage the arts and Germany was in a state of unrest, so it is to Italy with her rising generation of great painters, architects, sculptors and goldsmiths that one turns; and it is from Rome particularly, with the great Papal power as patron, that the revival comes, in this as in all the other arts.

At the beginning of the sixteenth century Rome inevitably had influence all over Europe. The religious divisions which have bedevilled Christianity since had barely appeared; the Papacy was perhaps the most potent political as well as religious force in Europe; and churchmen and laymen, visiting Rome in large numbers, could not fail to be strongly influenced by the colossal artistic upsurge we term the Renaissance. Florence, under the Medici, also had a well-founded tradition of goldsmiths' work; in fact, in that city a boy was invariably apprenticed to a goldsmith as a first step to practising any branch of the arts. Such towns as Venice, Siena, Milan, Bologna, Perugia, Naples and many other have records of flourishing bodies of goldsmiths during this period [figure 30]. Goldsmithing in Italy enjoyed the same consideration as the legal profession, and the prestige and influence of the worker were great. Between the Medici and the Papal Court, Italy attracted the best craftsmen Europe could produce, and both had regular establishments of goldsmiths. Records at this time show colossal orders. The Medici's vast establishment made a lavish use of secular plate, and religious silver and gold work for the Pontifical court was immense in its complexities, with presentation rings, swords, caps of state, tiaras, the golden roses which were presented to various rulers (Henry VIII of England is recorded as having received no fewer than three before his secession from Rome) and the large quantity of religious plate of every description. Rome in this century attracted all the great names, Benvenuto Cellini, Antonio Gentili, Valerio Belli and many others, some of whom had large workshops and many of whom came from the north. Most of their work has been lost and attributions where pieces have survived are difficult: as we have already seen, marking regulations in Rome were neither stringently enforced nor readily complied with, and unless signed the majority of these early pieces bear no mark. In addition,

21 A Chinese blue and white Ming porcelain jar with silver-gilt mounts, London, 1550

22 The famous gold salt-cellar made for Francis I of France by Cellini in 1543. It is the only remaining piece known without doubt to be from Cellini's hand

goldsmiths for centuries have worked to common designs — Michelangelo for instance is known to have produced these — and as a result, unless pieces are so individualistic as to be unmistakeable, definite ascriptions are not easy.

The Roman goldsmiths of the Renaissance were greatly influenced by ancient architects, sculptors and medallists, and their work as a result displays superb modelling of these particular features; their ability in equating figure and architectural forms is quite outstanding. Incorporated in virtually all their work at this time is outstanding enamelling, a distinct art and beautifully conceived to add brilliance to the goldsmith's product. Renaissance jewellery, a considerable quantity of which has survived, proves this abundantly. A feature of the Roman goldsmith is his versatility; Cellini, for instance, is famous as a sculptor and mentions himself that he undertook enam-

23 A German columbine-shaped cup made in Nuremberg in 1572. It is one of the known 'test' pieces made for admission to the guild

24 The Gibbon Salt, an Elizabeth I silver-gilt and crystal standing salt, 1576. These salts were the most important table ornaments at an Elizabethan banquet

25 (left) A German double-cup of silver-gilt and crystal, Strasbourg, c. 1550

elling, overcome with admiration at another's work. He was also a medallist and jeweller, and it is certain that he was not unique in his versatility [figure 5]. Not much sixteenth-century secular work has survived, but as one would expect, there is a considerable quantity of religious silver. Realistic figure-modelling on crosses, reliquaries, chalices, coffers, candlesticks, altar backs and other church accessories, cast, chased, engraved and decorated with colourful enamelling (with a considerable use of crystal) are characteristic of this period. Cellini has probably achieved the greatest fame, largely as a result of his

21

26 A German silver-gilt cup and cover, Augsburg, *c.* 1550

entertaining memoirs which every student of the Italian Renaissance should read. Evidently a brilliant but undeniably conceited artist, his description of the pieces which he and others produced makes somewhat depressing reading, for it emphasises the quantity of magnificent work which has been lost. The only item known for certain to be from Cellini's hand is the gold salt cellar he made for Francis I of France [figure 22]. The history of this is worth re-telling. Originally ordered by Cardinal Ippolito d'Este of Ferrara in 1539, it was modelled in wax, but when Cellini entered the service of the King of France in 1540 it was finally completed for the latter three years later. Cellini was overwhelmed with commissions in Paris and his statue *The Nymph of Fontainebleau* may still be seen in the Louvre. Only nineteen years after its completion, in 1562, the gold salt with other objects from the Royal Treasury was ordered to be melted to raise funds, at the time of the first outbreak of civil war between Catholics and Huguenots, but by sheer luck it escaped this fate and was given in 1570 to Archduke Ferdinand of the Tyrol. It subsequently found its way into the Ambras Collection and is now preserved in the Vienna Kunstindustrie museum. Cellini described his salt in great detail in his biography. It is oval, mounted with a figure of Neptune and the goddess Tellus, the former supported by sea-horses with an oval bowl in the form of a ship at his left hand for the salt, the latter with a small Ionic temple for holding pepper at her right hand, resting on flowers, fruit and animals, all standing on an oval base with symbolic figures. Much of the delicate enamel has now disappeared. It is in every respect a magnificent example of beautiful modelling and technical skill, and yet somehow, a little ill-balanced: one feels that the gods might fall off their perches. Some authorities feel that Cellini, though technically superb, was not outstanding as a designer. In the early sixteenth century Italian goldsmiths' work emphasised graceful form based on their vast classical heritage; towards the end of the century, though no less skilful, line tended to become submerged by exuberant detail, foreshadowing the baroque style with its over-heavy ornament. Nonetheless we owe to the Italian goldsmiths of this period the complete break with medieval tradition, the superb ceremonial secular plate and the entirely new styles, fashions and techniques which spread via Germany, the Low Countries and France to England [figure 32].

The advent of the Baroque in Italy combined with less active patronage of the arts moved the sphere of goldsmiths' influence to Germany, above all to Augsburg and Nuremberg, which had been rivalling Rome since the middle of the century. The Germans seemed reluctant to discard the existing Gothic forms in their church plate and it is in their secular silver that the influence of the Renaissance is most widely seen. Augsburg and Nuremberg, as much as Rome, were extremely wealthy cosmopolitan cities, and the goldsmiths there were freely patronised by ecclesiastics, princes and nobles. There are more fine secular pieces of German silver of this date in existence than Italian: wider dispersal of their products as well as

27 An Elizabeth I Magdalen cup, London, 1573

28 An English Tigerware jug by William Cater, London, 1571

23

29 With the voyages of exploration in the late fifteenth century, globe cups became fashionable: a Swiss globe cup by Abraham Gessner, Zurich, c. 1580

a far greater volume from their workshops probably accounts for this. Apart from purely ornamental silver, of which there was a great deal, the chief pieces to have survived in any quantity are drinking vessels, tankards, beakers and cups of every description. It is dangerous to generalise on form, but the tapered cylindrical or bell-shaped bowl seems to have been most common. The cups and covered tankards are decorated with *repoussé* so-called 'pineapple' lobing (a typically Germanic form of decoration particularly prevalent in Nuremberg), circular bosses or chased masks and scroll designs [figures 50, 52]. Standing cups incorporating crystal were made, and double-cups which are a peculiarly German form, both footed, the upper rim fitting into the lower, and which were made in considerable quantity during the century [figure 25]. Equally so are various forms of small beaker, originally made in pairs, dozens and half-dozens from about 1550 for approximately a century. Some, with projecting moulded girdles, fit one inside the other. The subjects on these little beakers, often beautifully engraved or chased, may deal with episodes for each month of the year or with hunting, scriptural and allegorical subjects [figure 42]. The German engraver or chaser was particularly prone to use biblical scenes from both the Old and the New Testaments. Lutheranism in Germany in the middle of the century made the local silversmith less likely than ever to use figures of saints or any forms which could be described as idolatrous. Other typically German pieces were the ornate and extremely large cups and covers, intended purely for display. The size of some of them is quite remarkable. Tankards were relatively simple, generally tapered, cylindrical or panelled with chased or embossed decoration. A small amount of filigree work is to be found at the end of the century, and coconuts are occasionally found mounted in silver, though unlike his English counterpart, the German goldsmith rarely lavished outstanding work on these pieces. Cups and tankards in mother-of-pearl, silver mounted, were also made; in North Germany amber tankards were mounted in silvergilt and late in the century a rather tall cylindrical tankard was produced in the Baltic area.

A fresh development were cups formed as terrestrial or celestial globes, generally with magnificently modelled figure stems and finials and finely engraved bowls [figures 29, 40]. Cups formed as figures of birds and animals began

30 The Italian love of the grotesque is well shown by this Venetian silver-gilt ewer and basin, *c.* 1580

to be made also, but did not become common until the following century, although a few groups of Diana and the stag have survived. Guild cups appeared in great numbers from the earliest times: every craft had its guild, and almost every town-guild, however small, its standing cup, which was passed from hand to hand as a loving cup.

In the last quarter of the seventeenth century German goldsmiths' work became really outstanding. Already masters of plate for display, the ewers and dishes, coolers, *tazze*, salvers and the innumerable other requisites in silver which the wealthy patron might commission poured out of the Augsburg and Nuremberg workshops. Figure modelling equalled, and perhaps some even surpassed, the best Italy had produced. In these decades even in England German pattern books and techniques gave silver an impression almost entirely German. Richness of visual appearance was the aspiration of the goldsmith: surfaces were entirely decorated; ewers, basins and dishes cast and chased in bold relief with mythological and biblical scenes, cups and tankards *repoussé* and chased with strapwork, swags of fruit and flower sprays with stamped and skilfully tooled borders. German silver may be considered by many too flamboyant, even over-decorated, but no one can deny its magnificence [figures 35, 41, 44, 50, 52].

31 In an age when forks were rarities, ewers were a necessity for washing the hands after meals. A German silver-gilt rose-water ewer and dish by Hans Ment, Augsburg, c. 1580

32 An Italian silver-gilt dish from Genoa, *c.* 1580

Perhaps it is worth noting briefly that in Germany the salt cellar never attained the importance in this century that it did in England. German salts on the whole are small and triangular and are not lavished with the skilled work reserved for other ceremonial pieces.

As in Italy, the century produced some outstanding craftsmen; in Nuremberg there were Wenzel Jamnitzer, who with his brother Albrecht and their sons carried on a flourishing business [figure 40], Cristoff Ritter and the Ritter family, Melchior Baier and many others.

Augsburg goldsmiths flourished also, though individual workers there in the sixteenth century do not appear to have made such reputations. Of these craftsmen, Wenzel Jamnitzer holds the status in Germany that Cellini held in Rome. Unlike Cellini, a considerable number of pieces ascribed to Jamnitzer have survived, and like the Italian,

33 (*far left*) An Elizabethan standing salt, height 12 ins, London, 1589

34 (*left*) An Elizabethan silver-gilt gourd-shaped cup and cover, London, 1596

35 (*right*) A German silver-gilt *tazza*, made in Augsburg, *c.* 1585. This was one of a set of twelve and was formerly one of the Aldobrandini heirlooms

36 An Elizabeth I cup and cover of silver-gilt and mother-of-pearl, London, 1590

37 This Elizabeth I silver-gilt tankard by John Harryson, London, 1580, shows considerable German influence.

he made skilled use of fine enamelling. His working life in Nuremberg was a long one: a native of Vienna where he was born in 1508, he became master-goldsmith in 1534 and did not die until 1585. His products were evidently deeply influenced by contemporary Italian design, although he may be criticized for minute ornamentation; he literally encrusted some of his works with insects, lizards etc.

What Jamnitzer brought the Nuremberg goldsmiths was that attention to detail carried through to absolute perfection at which the German craftsman has always been so adept. Like Cellini, when employed on his work, he spared nothing. Both as a designer and a craftsman his influence on South German goldsmiths' work was great, and fortunately ewers and basins, caskets, cups, an exquisite set of four figure candlesticks depicting the seasons, and other pieces from his hand are still extant. As always, apart from actual technical competence, a great deal of the ascendancy of German work had to do with the designers, and in this century three others particularly had considerable influence, Virgil Solis of Nuremberg, Hans Brosamer and Georg Wechter.

In England the long and bitter Wars of the Roses, which ended in 1488, had not affected the London Goldsmiths' Guild in that it had instituted marking regulations and a system of date-letters, but it must inevitably have had an adverse effect on the trade as a whole, as did a century of war with France. Medieval England, like the rest of the continent, had produced ecclesiastical and secular silver of the Gothic type, little of which has survived, but of no markedly national characteristics. No native Cellini or Jamnitzer appears in the London records during the course of the century, and the craft is particularly dependent on foreign influences and one suspects on foreign workmen. Certainly the inventories of the Royal Plate in Tudor times, recently annotated, show a considerable proportion of foreign silver from Germany, France, Flanders and elsewhere.

England in many ways suffered a far greater religious revolution (when Henry VIII suppressed the monasteries in 1536) than any country on the continent. Due to his measures and the Civil War which occurred in the following century, there is almost no sixteenth-century and earlier Church plate available, compared with the relatively large amount in Italy and elsewhere. Nor was the unsettled state of the Church during the course of the century likely

38 A German silver-gilt wagercup, Nuremberg, c. 1600

39 An Elizabethan Bell salt, London, 1600. Bell salts were peculiar to England

to warrant fresh commissions from the clergy, who were such patrons of the goldsmiths in Germany and Italy; indeed by the middle of the century the Church had been instructed to use a very limited amount of plate and the rest had been confiscated. What Church plate there was generally dated from the previous century and was almost entirely medieval in character. The few pieces of early sixteenth-century secular plate which survive still show strong medieval influence. Where figures are used (which is rare in the early part of the century) they are crude except for isolated examples. As in Germany, the majority of pieces to survive are drinking vessels; maple-wood bowls, mounted in silver, were made up to the middle of the sixteenth century, but ceased to be produced when other forms of cup were made. One of the most popular of these was font-shaped, made for some seventy-five years, and as such can perhaps fairly be described as a national form. Cups and tankards, very akin to the German, were made in considerable quantity towards the end of the century, and ostrich eggs, coconuts, shells and even the German stoneware jugs were mounted in silver with some care, a fact which surprised more than one foreign visitor [figure 37]. Newly imported bowls, bottles, flagons and jugs of Chinese porcelain were similarly mounted, as was crystal, believed to detect poison [figure 21]. In general the English goldsmith·did not decorate his work as profusely as his German counterpart, nor, it must be admitted, as well. Although superficially *repoussé* work and chasing may appear similar, close examination of comparable German and English work of the same date will reveal a difference in finish. The Elizabethan goldsmith in England was able to achieve a very rich effect by the stamping of borders and by other methods, but scrupulous and meticulous attention to detail were not his forte nor was he able to produce comparable cast work. Salts, hour-glass shaped, cylindrical, quadrangular, in architectural forms, and at the end of the century bell-shaped, are of considerable importance in England, occupying the place of honour on a banqueting table [figures 24, 33, 39]. Ewers and basins also were produced in the latter part of the century in increased numbers, but apart from a pleasing individuality in outline, they are not comparable with the best German and Italian work [figure 15]. *Tazze*, **originating in Italy, through Germany and France, were also made in England, again not as flamboyantly decorated**

31

40 An ornamental globe made by Christoph Jamnitzer, a member of the famous goldsmith family, in Nuremberg, c. 1600. The globe shows the American continent

as the German but directly influenced [figure 6]. One particular piece which is so German as to be confusing is the gourd-shaped cup with figure finial, the stem formed as a tree-trunk with or without a diminutive figure of a woodcutter [figure 34]. Whether made by German craftsmen in that country and imported or merely made to German pattern books by Englishmen, they are frequently indistinguishable. Some cups have been found with both German and English hall-marks. Animal and bird forms, with the odd isolated exception, never found favour in England. Later in the century beakers appear, generally with restrained engraved decoration. There was also considerable Flemish influence with the direct trade between southern and eastern English ports and the continent, which becomes even more marked after 1600. Hans Holbein designed pieces of silver for Henry VIII; some of these designs have survived, but not, unhappily, the actual pieces. Reverting to church plate, a considerable number of chalices, patens, alms dishes and flagons were made in the last twenty years of the century and a number of the former have survived. Where English design does differ quite considerably from the German is in the proportion of unadorned pieces. English taste, with a few lapses, favours the predominantly simple form in silver, and even in the sixteenth century, when one would be faced with a difficult task indeed to find either Italian or German goldsmiths' work which was not heavily embellished and decorated, there tend in England to be a number of pieces relying entirely on simplicity and beauty of line, a trend even more greatly to be seen early in the following century [figure 58]. English goldsmiths never in any case attained the tremendous exuberance we find in Italy and Germany at the end of the century, rather their tendency for more restrained forms became more marked.

The history of France at this time is an involved and troubled one. The previous century with its civil disturbances and long, crippling war with England was scarcely conducive to demand for and growth of the goldsmiths' technique. The sixteenth century showed little improvement: in the last four decades there were no fewer than eight civil wars, mostly between Huguenots and Catholics, involving latterly a struggle for the throne. As a result, the regrettably few pieces of silver which have survived the melting pot show as strong medieval charac-

41 A German silver-gilt *tazza*, Augsburg, *c.* 1590. Augsburg and Nuremberg were the two great silver-making centres of Germany

teristics as in England, and although the foreign artists brought in by Francis I must have injected fresh vitality into the craft, these forms continue, particularly in some provincial examples, throughout the century and even into the next. Cellini's masterpiece made for the French King, the gold salt already described, barely avoided being melted less than twenty years after its completion and under the conditions prevailing throughout their reigns, Charles IX, Henry III, and the Catholic and Huguenot nobility, must have had a constant drain on their resources necessitating the frequent conversion of what plate they possessed into coin. We have to rely on contemporary inventories and designs rather than surviving pieces to get some idea of French design at this time.

Late medieval in form until about 1530, there are then signs that the Italian Renaissance was beginning to have some effect on French design and from the time that Francis I attracted Italians to Paris, that influence de-

42 (*left*) A silver-gilt standing cup and cover by Nichlas Rapp, Ulm, *c.* 1580.
(*centre*) A silver-gilt and *niello* 'Monatsbecher' by Hans Uten, Nuremberg, *c.* 1620.
(*right*) A silver-gilt standing cup and cover by Michel Flindt, Nuremberg, *c.* 1570

43 This James I dessert stand, London, 1619, shows Portuguese influence

veloped and one reads of richly decorated work, cast, embossed, chased, engraved and enamelled, the French proving apt pupils of their Italian teachers. That the trade did not languish completely after the outbreak of the first civil disturbances is proved by the fact that Henry III found it necessary to impose a tax on silver in 1579 to discourage the melting of coin to furnish domestic silver, a practice which in France and other countries caused a serious shortage of currency at particular periods. This would seem to indicate that silver was being turned into

35

the same magnificent, opulent pieces we find elsewhere in Europe, but scarcely a piece remains, and towards the end of the century, with religious persecution and the constant disruption caused by domestic dissent, French goldsmiths were again migrating to Flanders and elsewhere.

It is impossible, in studying influence on goldsmiths' work in this century and a half, to ignore that of Flanders and Holland. Antwerp, Bruges, Ghent, Liège, Amsterdam, Dordrecht, the Hague, Utrecht and many other towns had guilds, makers' marks and date-letter systems, many being superior to those we have already studied, of comparable antiquity and prestige. Antwerp, under the influence of the Dukes of Burgundy, had become the focal point of European trade in the mid-sixteenth century, rivalling Rome as a centre of the arts, with its flourishing school of painters, attracting craftsmen of all kinds, particularly those from France who found it a haven after the turbulent state of affairs in their own country. With England just across the water carrying on a flourishing trade with the Low Countries, one detects some similarity in the silver of the two early in the sixteenth century, but by 1550 German influence, as in England, became dominant. Like Germany, a beer and wine drinking country, it is drinking vessels of all types which have survived in greatest quantities in the Netherlands. Towards the end of the century, the influence which Antwerp exerted as a leader of world trade declined and shifted northwards to the United Provinces, which after the revolt against Spanish rule which had lasted for thirteen years and culminated in the Union of Utrecht in 1579, had declared their sovereignty in 1584. Antwerp, on the other hand, was sacked twice in eight years, in 1576 by the Spanish and in 1583 by the French. The Dutch were not slow to seize the advantages offered and in a remarkably short time became the great world sea-power, a position they retained for a good century and a half. Both the Dutch East and West Indian Companies were founded in the early seventeenth century, trade expanded colossally, the country became prosperous and as a natural corollary the arts flourished: fine schools of architecture and painting sprang up, and allied to these were the other arts including goldsmithing.

A considerable number of fine pieces from the late sixteenth and early seventeenth centuries are extant, and

44 *left* A German silver-gilt cup and cover made in Nuremberg, *c.* 1595

the Dutch have a number which if not peculiar to them, survive in greater quantity in Holland than elsewhere. Guild-minded like the Germans, they made a large number of guild shields and cups. Plaques, ewers and basins, *tazze*, dishes, beakers and cups of all kinds are the principal survivals. The Dutch goldsmith was a master of the

45 A hexagonal German standing salt made in Worms in the early seventeenth century. Large standing salts were rare in Germany

46 The Myddleton Cup, an Elizabeth I silver-gilt standing cup, London, 1599, plainer than the cup from Nuremberg

47 Two German parcel-gilt tankards, *above* Augsburg *c.* 1650, and *below* Danzig, *c.* 1650

technique of embossing: even the minutely decorated plaques which abound are rarely ·cast, but are far more frequently embossed and engraved. Renaissance-inspired ornament was the dominant influence on work at the turn of the century but subsequently a unique style developed which had an effect on design in other countries. In this the Dutch goldsmith was influenced by goldsmiths, painters and engravers in his own and other countries, Cellini, the Jamnitzer family, Virgil Solis, Albrecht Dürer, Titian and many others. The most unusual and typical development in style in the early seventeenth century was the use of the grotesque mask, not strictly defined, but merely giving the impression of a face, either human or animal. At the same time dolphins and all forms of grotesque sea creatures were introduced, and latterly lobing was very widely used. Prior to about 1620 Renaissance decoration with its exactitude of outline and clearly defined form was adhered to, but with the introduction of these other designs, definition of form and outline became less pronounced and a more flowing, flexible style came into fashion. As practised by a really talented goldsmith this decoration is delightful: in less competent work it loses its effect.

Like Italy and Germany Holland produced its outstanding craftsmen, the most famous of whom were Adam and Paul Van Vianen and Johannes Lutma, Adam, working between approximately 1594 and his death in 1627 while his brother Paul died in 1613. The latter worked in Italy, Munich and Prague for most of his life; Adam is believed never to have left the country. Both were masters of superb naturalistic embossed landscapes with figures in the foregound, initially of secondary importance but later dominating the composition. Both worked largely from Dutch engravings and German plaques. By the second decade of the seventeenth century Adam had developed the extraordinary flowing grotesques which were further developed by his son, the second Adam, whose designs exaggerated his father's style still more. This tended to produce a somewhat ill defined technique, particularly when indifferently carried out. The effects of these designs can be clearly seen in later German and English work. The other really outstanding development in Holland in this century is the superlative engraving. By 1650 beakers, boxes, the polygonal dishes so peculiarly Dutch, the cups and any other form of plate which present-

48 This Commonwealth tankard by James Plummer, York, 1649, is inscribed with edifying texts. 'Judge as thou wouldst be judged', 'Be faithful till death', and others

49 A French gold and crystal cup made in 1620. Crystal was thought to detect the presence of poison

ed a suitable surface were being engraved with architectural, harbour, hunting, fishing and other scenes, with shipping, human figures, animals, birds and fruit clusters, floral and foliate sprays and every conceivable subject [figure 51]. The delicacy, skill and beauty of these lovely designs are well worth studying in detail as a casual glance often fails to reveal the touches which made the engraved subject such a perfect composite whole. The similarity of engraving found on English and French work from about 1660 onwards and on German at an earlier date points to Dutch engravers in these countries. It is possibly the peak period of the silver engraver's art.

Although by 1650 Holland was becoming the predominant influence on European styles and techniques, at the turn of the century it was still Germany which remained supreme. The first half-century saw little basic change in the type of piece produced: animal models, various beakers, individually and in sets, tankards and cups were made, if anything in larger quantities than hitherto. The pineapple decoration during these fifty years reached its peak [figure 52]. Wager-cups, generally the figure of a woman, her skirt forming the bowl and holding a smaller pivoted cup above her head, continued to be made; these had first been introduced towards the end of the previous century. Ostrich shells, nautilus shells and coconuts were still mounted in silver. As the century progressed, more engraving was to be found, together with more use of foliate ornament, both probably the effect of Dutch work. In general tankards and cups were of a fairly thin gauge of metal, the *repoussé* work employed having a stiffening effect. Some pieces towards the middle of the century were found, predominantly plain but with pounced or matted decoration over most of the surface, found more frequently after 1660, a trend exactly the reverse of that in England where this decoration was found early in the century.

English style and ornament during this half-century is more divorced from German design, the tendency being for domestic silver to become plainer and simpler as opposed to the rather ornate decorative forms still widely employed in Germany. The oviform cup with a curious steeple finial, confined to England, begins to appear, and wine cups also, which have distinctly national characteristics, are made [figures 55, 58]. Formal floral and foliate ornament, quite divorced from the fruit swag and

39

50 (*left*) A German silver-gilt tankard, *c.* 1600

51 A Dutch silver-gilt octagonal dish, width 10½ ins, Delft, *c.* 1650. The Dutch were the foremost engravers of the age

52 (*right*) A German silver-gilt 'pineapple' cup and cover, Nuremberg, *c.* 1615

53 A Commonwealth sexfoil cup and cover, London, c. 1650

strapwork of German inspired designs, is used, and *repoussé* work becomes less favoured. With the beginning of the third decade of the century a preference for preponderantly plain plate evinces itself, relieved only by matting, if at all. Tankards and cups tend to become simpler until by 1640 they achieve a supremely severe line, often beautifully balanced but in many cases somewhat crudely finished [figures 48, 53]. Due partly no doubt to some scarcity of silver as a result of the Civil War, an extraordinarily light gauge is found from about 1630 to 1655, relieved by a certain amount of very crude and poor relief work in the form of punched dots, lines and tendrils. Engraving too is execrable compared with the Dutch, beside which it looks extremely amateurish. The only interesting developments are the effect of Portuguese work on some English pieces [figure 43], which has been proved, and the existence of good engraving in the Scandinavian taste, found on some East Anglian pieces. Apart from the plain examples which can be admired for beauty of line, the English goldsmiths' product reached a low ebb at this time; some slightly improved *repoussé* work appears shortly before the restoration of Charles II, an indication of the return of the ornate and flamboyant work which is the feature of his reign.

This long period of one hundred and fifty years, in which the influences of different countries in turn upon European goldsmiths' work can be followed, is succeeded by one, almost equally long, in which a single country, France, is particularly dominant. The paucity of silver from the middle of the seventeenth century is not so marked; for silver became more widely used by a larger cross-section of society and, as a result, more personal and interesting.

French Influence in Europe 1660-1730

54 This German eagle by Heinrich Mannlich, Augsburg, *c.* 1690, was purely ornamental

MUCH OF THE SILVER ALREADY DESCRIBED and discussed has a purely academic interest for the reader, as very little European silver prior to the middle of the seventeenth century is to be found, except in museum collections where it is out of circulation for ever. Magnificent though national museum displays may be, works of art on view inevitably lose some of their distinctiveness, massed as they are in glass cases. This is particularly so in the case of silver, so complementary to its contemporary furnishing and back-

ground. Silver, like porcelain, is designed to be used, handled and appreciated in the setting for which it was intended, and the constant steady drain of pieces to museum collections, though understandable and inevitable, is (solely from this viewpoint) unfortunate. However from the middle of the seventeenth century a large amount of domestic silver can be found and in addition, with its greatly increased use in all spheres of society, we find for the first time small pieces still made today which are eminently practical besides being beautiful.

The year 1660 marks two events which have considerable bearing on goldsmiths' work. In England, after eleven years of the Protectorate, the monarchy was restored in the person of Charles II. In France, Louis XIV, who attained his majority in 1651, married the Infanta Maria Theresa and shortly afterwards Colbert began to reorganise French finances with a considerable measure of success.

Although Dutch goldsmiths remained the dominant influence in European work for another decade or two, it was in France that the most remarkable transition in the state of the craft took place. The glittering court which shortly established itself at Versailles, the personal government of the King, with his love of luxury and lavish living, and the improved financial position which was the direct result of Colbert's reforms all contributed to a more extravagant way of life, and it was the goldsmith particularly who benefited from this. The court, the nobility, the church and the rich merchant classes who were beginning to emerge, all placed orders with the Paris goldsmith. The pieces he made at this period are of every conceivable kind, frequently lavishly decorated in contrast to some of the rather severe styles of the earlier half of the century, relieved only by frugal ornament. This is the period of the massive suites of silver-covered furniture, a few exceptions being of solid metal, the candle-stands, mirrors and andirons, all in silver; chandeliers, candelabra, wall-sconces, and candlesticks, bathing the colourful rooms in a mellow light, beautiful toilet services with ewers and basins, dressing table candlesticks, bottles, boxes, brushes and every conceivable toilet appliance, lavished on the wives and mistresses of the wealthy. Dining tables groaned beneath a mass of silver; plates, dishes, tureens, wine cisterns and coolers and other pieces too diverse to list.

Forms of ornament, influenced more perhaps by the Netherlands than any other country, also changed. The

55 (*opposite*) A Charles I steeple cup and cover, London, 1627. The cup is engraved with waves, in which some cheerful dolphins are swimming

56 A Charles II silver-gilt ewer, height 8 ins, London, 1671

57 A Charles II salver on a single foot, London, 1660, shows hunting-scenes

58 (*right*) This James I wine cup, made in London in 1617, is severely plain compared to continental silver of the same date

59 The famous Lennoxlove toilet service, a French silver-gilt service made in Paris, 1660–1677. Most of it bears the monogram and coronet of Frances Stuart, Duchess of Richmond and Lennox (1647–1702)

predominantly plain designs previously adhered to had meant that the current generation of goldsmiths had lost much of the ability to execute adequate *repoussé* work or engraved decoration. As a result workers were attracted from other countries and one finds a number of foreigners in Paris recorded from this time, Dutchmen, Germans and others. The principal form of decoration presumably originally inspired by the Dutch flower and leaf designs, is ornate scrolling and floral and foliate *repoussé* and chased work, often with armorial engraving as well. This ornament develops as a distinct form, with little affinity to the Dutch, in tight formal scrolls and boldly sweeping

60 A Louis XIV wall-sconce, Paris, c. 1680

61 *Chinoiserie* engraving came in at the Restoration, and was particularly popular in England. A punch-bowl by Benjamin Pyne, London, c. 1680

flower sprays, with the addition of *amorini* or *putti* on occasion. Ornate, but beautifully executed all-over decoration remained in vogue for some fifteen or twenty years together with simpler, heavier designs which later became more fashionable, lasting for thirty years and producing some of the loveliest forms in silver that the goldsmith has achieved in any age or country. Engraving also, particularly on the smaller pieces, became a highly developed art, and here too one suspects Dutch influence and even engravers, for some of their seventeenth-century engraving, as we have already seen, is as beautiful as any ever produced. One particularly encounters this delicate work on the stems of forks and spoons [figure 13].

Inconceivable though it may seem, the surviving pieces of French silver of this period, though greater than those of previous centuries, are remarkably few, and two really magnificent toilet services would undoubtedly have been melted had they not been preserved in England. One is known as the Lennoxlove toilet service, now in the Royal Scottish Museum, Edinburgh [figure 59]; the other silver-gilt, is in the possession of the Duke of Devonshire. The former belonged to Frances, Duchess of Lennox, a famous beauty at the court of Charles II; the latter, engraved with the monogram of William of Orange and Mary, daughter of James II, who subsequently became joint monarchs of England in 1688, was probably acquired by them on their marriage in 1677, taken to Holland and thence to England. A French table, covered in silver, c. 1680, is also preserved in England, at Osterley Park, Isleworth. These apart, the bulk of the superb silver of all kinds which is known to have been made was sacrificed to provide money to finance the costly wars at the end of the century, that of the League of Augsburg, when France in 1689 was opposed by Germany, England, Spain, Denmark and Savoy, and the even more ruinous war of the Spanish Succession from 1701 until the Treaty of Utrecht in 1713. Not only did Louis XIV melt most of the Royal plate; he instructed his subjects to make the same sacrifices and unfortunately his orders were all too well carried out. It must be remembered, too, that the tax on silver, already briefly mentioned, was introduced in 1672 specifically to discourage the conversion of coin into domestic plate, and this must have had a restraining effect on the production at least of some of the more costly pieces.

62 The popularity of silver furniture lasted longest in Germany and Scandinavia: a large German mirror by Albrecht Biller, Augsburg, 1680

Parallel with the development of the French goldsmith's technique runs that of his English equivalent. England, with its recent Civil War of 1642-1649, followed by eleven years of puritanical rule, was ripe for a change. The unnatural restraint imposed by the Puritans caused a violent swing at the Restoration of Charles II to a richer, more colourful way of life, to which the goldsmith readily adapted his styles. Already showing some restrained return to crude embossed decoration, Dutch and French influence, allied with the luxurious and exuberant fashions which the King introduced, caused a radical and rapid change in design [figure 57]. 1666, the year of the great fire of London, also marked Huguenot persecution in France, and although England was at that time at war with France, peace was concluded the following year and from this time a constant stream of Huguenot craftsmen of all kinds entered the country, far-sightedly encouraged by the King. Charles also brought a considerable number of foreigners with him on his return, and was the recipient only a few years afterwards of a plea from the London goldsmiths complaining of their neglect in favour of the 'multitude of strangers', asking him to restrict the activities of foreign craftsmen. Fortunately for English design, these requests were ignored and the majority of outstanding goldsmiths at the turn of the century and shortly afterwards are of French Huguenot origin. The rebuilding of the city of London after the fire was accompanied by a brisk demand for the latest goldsmith's work, and the arts in general flourished.

England, even more than France, found herself with a generation of goldsmiths who had little skill in the delicate and intricate *repoussé* work which came into fashion and there is little doubt that foreign goldsmiths, who no doubt proved more skilled at these techniques, were well patronised and aroused the antagonism of native craftsmen. For the first ten or fifteen years of the reign the principal influence was Dutch: silver of a fairly light gauge was still used and the *repoussé* work on porringers, salvers and similar pieces tends to be of reasonably naturalistic flowers of poppy, tulip and lily types interspersed sometimes with somewhat crude animal figures or occasionally birds, rarely human, though masks comparable with those carved on contemporary woodwork do appear [figure 73]. Armorial engraving is quite neat, but not outstanding and in no way comparable with the delicate Dutch engraving. Combined with these is the use of lobed decoration, less

63 The Seymour Salt, a Charles II rock-crystal and silver-gilt salt, made in London, *c.* 1662; the property of the Worshipful Company of Goldsmiths

imaginatively employed than by the Dutch, and the occasional rare example employing the Dutch grotesque popularised by the Van Vianen family. Christian, the son of Adam Van Vianen, was in England in 1637, employed by Charles I to make the chapel plate at Windsor (melted in the Civil War) and believed to be the executor also of some excellent portrait medallions. The Van Vianen designs were engraved by Van Kessel in 1641 and must

49

64 (*left*) A Dutch cup and cover, height 12½ ins, by Deventer, *c.* 1695.

(*centre*) A Swiss pineapple cup and cover by H. J. Bullinger II, Zurich, 1665.

(*right*) A German silver-gilt cup and cover, Frankenthal, *c.* 1670

have had some effect on English work subsequently. In all fairness though, it must be admitted that a great deal of English goldsmiths' work fell well below that of their Dutch contemporaries although by the time the French fashions became the primary influence, their technique had improved immeasurably. By 1675 the naturalistic Dutch-inspired decoration had been largely replaced by the French acanthus and formal foliate ornament and indeed English toilet services are in existence which are remarkably akin to their French counterparts, but when one considers that the number of French Huguenot refugees working in London at this time must have been quite

65 A pair of German table candlesticks by Johannes Mittnacht, Augsburg, c. 1680

considerable, it is hardly surprising. As a direct result of trade in the East, one delightful and wholly English form of engraving, which appears between approximately 1680 and 1690 and then ceases abruptly, is what is known as *Chinoiserie* decoration, an extraordinarily naïve use of imaginary oriental figures, exotic birds, plants and trees [figure 61]. It is particularly appealing and never palls, appearing on toilet services, tankards, salvers, caskets and every conceivable form of plate [figure 80]. Curiously enough it is entirely absent from Dutch silver, and less surprisingly from French. The pieces on which this decoration appears as a rule have more body than hitherto and after its demise the simple forms appear employing a heavier gauge still with a minimum of decoration, a direct off-shoot of the French style.

A list of the various types of domestic articles found in England during this period would be almost identical to those briefly mentioned at Louis XIV's court, but the difference lies in the survival of a much greater quantity.

Reverting to France, which throughout this century and a half was always a few years ahead of England, the last two decades of the seventeenth century saw a development of an essentially new style, one which relied on simplicity of outline, together with a minimum of restrained decoration or virtually none at all. This had in fact been running parallel with the more ornate *repoussé* work; latterly this was abandoned completely and plain designs, employing far more metal, took the field. The most typical decorative addition at this time is 'cut-card' work, which exists in fact as early as 1660 and continues to be used in a variety of forms until about 1730. So called because of its similarity to cardboard, it is thin sheet silver applied generally to the lower halves of bodies of cups or beakers, salver bases, saucepan handles, *écuelle* covers and similar pieces. Certainly one of the most attractive ornamental techniques conceived by the goldsmith, it is one aspect of the fashion for rather intricate decoration which was used, and included the use of small applied medallions, classically inspired. Light decorative engraving and the wide use of simple gadroon borders are forms which lasted until about 1730, though as the eighteenth century advanced this decoration becomes a little more insistent and the fine simplicity of form somewhat subordinated to it, a trait which is not apparent in the really plain silver of the previous half century. It is fairly certain that until

66 A rare pair of Scottish tankards by James Cockburn, Edinburgh, 1685

the signing of the Treaty of Utrecht in 1713, the Paris goldsmiths had passed through an unsettled period, with the universal melting of silver in 1689 and again in 1709. What is quite certain is the disastrous effect of the Revocation of the Edict of Nantes in 1685, which proved calamitous to French industry for a period, causing as it did the almost wholesale emigration of the hard-working Huguenot population, including a number of goldsmiths.

Although most forms of French plate have their counterpart in England, there is one which is typically French, in the same way that steeple-cups were peculiar to England and pineapple cups were virtually confined to Germany. This is the covered *écuelle* or shallow circular porringer, often with a stand or dish, which is encountered from about 1660 onwards and continued to be made to the end of the period covered by this book [figure 78]. The bodies were generally plain in the seventeenth century, and the cover, practically flat, lent itself readily to the cut-card designs described, generally of swirling leaves in the early examples, later in more formal designs, and as the eighteenth century progressed, the cover was domed and chased, or engraved decoration became common. A feature of these *écuelles* which is imitated on covers of English pieces is the coiled snake finial, cast and applied. This is found both in France and England between about 1665 and 1680. Curiously, although with only a single handle and without any cover, the American porringer is much more akin to the French, though the former is far smaller, and they were made in America during the same period in the same large quantities. The little bell-shaped beakers which are also common remain a typically French form, so often exquisitely decorated with cut-card work and delicate engraving; it is strange that they were never made by the Huguenot goldsmiths in England, but with a general consumption of beer rather than wines, (borne out by the numbers of tankards and mugs which abound, compared with the quite small number of tapered cylindrical beakers and the general use of good native glass), it is perhaps not surprising.

As Paris goldsmiths' work suffers from the constricting influence and effects of war at the turn of the century, it may be more instructive to turn once again to their London counterparts and see to what extent workers of French descent had affected design and had become firmly established. The revocation of the Treaty of Nantes

67 A German silver-gilt salver by Johann
Ludwig Biller I, Augsburg, c. 1705

in 1685, as we have already seen, caused a second and greater influx of Huguenot goldsmiths to London, where a number were already established, and there is little doubt that by the real excellence of their work, allied probably with the lower rates for manufacture which they were forced to charge initially through sheer necessity, they rapidly established themselves. There are a number of complaints by the native London goldsmiths at this time, some of whom, (particularly those who were unwilling or unable to adopt the new techniques) may have been forced out of business. Records of the makers' marks at the London Goldsmiths' Hall, having survived the Great Fire of 1666, were unhappily destroyed subsequently, and only those from 1696 have been preserved. In these we find the names of Pierre Platel, Simon Pantin, Pierre Harache, David Willaume, Louis Cuny, Isaac Liger

68 (*above*) An American Caudle cup and cover by Gerrit Onkelbag (1670–1732), New York, *c.* 1690

69 (*above, right*) An American covered sugar box by Edward Winslow (1669–1753), Boston, *c.* 1702

70 An American tankard by Johannes Nys (1671–1734), Philadelphia, *c.* 1714. The engraving shows the cypher of James and Sarah Logan, married in 1714. James was secretary to William Penn

and many others with, in the early eighteenth century, those of Augustine Courtauld and Paul de Lamerie, the most famous of them all.

The wide use of domestic silver, unsequestrated as in France, is shown by the fact that in 1697 it was found necessary to raise the standard of silver above that of the coinage, a measure calculated, like the tax in France, to prevent direct melting of the currency. At the same time (so frequent had robberies in inns and taverns become because of the quantity of silver used in them) it was found necessary to ban its use in these places—an indication of the widespread use of the metal. The period from 1700 to 1730, as in France, is one which for sheer beauty of form has never been surpassed. Some of the pieces, particularly the more ornamental, like wine cisterns and coolers and some of the smaller items as well [figures 82, 77], could easily be French, and one literally has to look at the marks to establish a certain provenance. Most work is identifiably English, although French designs and techniques are entirely dominant. One finds the same basic forms in ewers, decorated with cut-card work, and dishes; toilet services also bear marked similarities and the cast and chased work which is encountered is very French. Polygonal forms come into vogue for casters, teapots, tea-kettles, coffee pots and other pieces of plate [figure 80], together with the plain baluster and the tapered cylindrical. Much of this work relies on symmetry and perfection of outline alone, with only the slightest decorative work, less than in contemporary French work

71 A Queen Anne sideboard dish, height 2 ft, by John Chartier, London, 1707, engraved with the arms of Sir Edward Lawrence of St Ives, Gentleman Usher to Queen Anne and Member of Parliament for Stockbridge 1705–1710

72 One of a set of four Queen Anne wall-sconces by John Bodington, 1710. It is engraved with the arms of William Herbert, 2nd Earl of Powys, and his wife Mary Preston

which was already some fifteen or twenty years ahead of England. As the third decade of the century approaches, chasing is more widely employed and the severely plain pieces are less in evidence.

In England at this time the engraving, both armorial and decorative, became really outstanding [figure 71]. Engraving in England was very much a specialised art, and the Dutch, as we have noted, were the outstanding exponents and influence in the seventeenth century. English engraving in the latter part of this century is quite competent, and the names of one or two engravers at this time have survived, but it is not until we come to the work of Simon Gribelin, yet another Huguenot refugee, and his contemporaries, that engraving comparable with the best of any date is encountered. Gribelin, whose ancestors had been watchmakers, is believed to have come to England in about 1680, five years before the main stream of Huguenot immigration. He became a member of the Clockmakers' Company in 1686 and appears to have been largely occupied with the decoration of watches. This naturally involved intricate, meticulous and detailed work, and in the few pieces of silver known to be from Gribelin's hand the same traits apply, his pieces being magnificent examples of the engraver's art. He published two books of engravings in 1697 and 1700 which must have had some considerable influence upon the business, and as he did not die until 1733, a large amount of the fine decorative and armorial engraving during these thirty years may be from his hand. Unfortunately he rarely signed his work. In this sphere at least it must be admitted that English technique surpassed the French, who in most other respects preserved throughout a lighter, more delicate, touch, both in design and ornament.

Although this survey is not intended to cover the work of American silversmiths in any detail, it may be of interest to note the European influences on the development of the American craft. The early southern colonists tended to import all their silver, but in Boston, for many years the most flourishing town in the colonies, in the mid-seventeenth century there were established silversmiths of English origin; there were many, too, in New Amsterdam, or New York as it became. Dutch influence was reflected in design and decoration, complemented after 1664, when the English assumed control, by craftsmen from that country. They were reinforced by Walloon and Huguenot

73 A Charles II two-handled cup and cover,
c. 1670, with a turkey cock on it. Turkeys
were only introduced into England about a
hundred years earlier

74 (*left*) A German silver-gilt Pilgrim bottle
made in Augsburg, *c.* 1700

refugees from religious persecution in Europe who settled
in considerable numbers in the new world. As a result one
finds beakers and bowls in New York with typically Dutch
engraved decoration: the silver of New England on the
other hand reflects contemporary English styles in mugs,
tankards, beakers, boxes, casters, spoons etc. After 1700
English influence naturally became more dominant, but
a characteristic of American silver throughout the eighteenth century is its simplicity of line: the ornate Rococo
styles never found much favour. A number of silversmiths

75 A German silver-gilt and Meissen porcelain travelling tea-service by Esajas Busch, Augsburg, c. 1714

achieved work comparable with the best in Europe, John Hull, Robert Sanderson, John Cony, Jeremiah Dummer, members of the Burt family and the Reveres, father and son, to name a few in Boston. In New York there were Peter Van Dyck, Le Roux, the Boelen family, Schaats, Wynkoop, Onclebagh and many others, their names reflecting their Dutch, French Huguenot and other European origins.

Until the late seventeenth century German goldsmiths remained relatively unaffected by French design, and continued a strong native tradition of skill and craftsmanship. With the return of peace in 1648 they were once again the recipients of large orders. Many of the products from the latter half of the century are still in circulation;

76 A Queen Anne octagonal tea-service by Richard Watts, 1712. The earliest teapot extant was made in England in 1680

77 A pair of George I double-lipped sauce-boats

and certain trends and changes in design are noticeable. The little beakers of various kinds, which had remained fashionable for over a century, and the pineapple cups, of which the greater quantity were made in Nuremberg, ceased to be made in any number, although isolated examples of the latter continue to occur [figure 64]. Tankards, on the other hand, are made if anything in still greater profusion, *repoussé* or cast and chased with classical or biblical scenes as a general rule. Little sweet-meat dishes are also common, and also larger oval dishes, some of the latter of very light gauge, embossed and chased with figure subjects, flowers and leaves, inspired by similar Dutch work. This influence becomes more marked towards the end of the century, when tankards, beakers and dishes are embossed with stylised floral and foliate ornament, not as skilfully executed as the Dutch but with closer affinity to the English, though better worked on the whole. The mania for cups in the form of all sorts of animals, at its strongest in the first half

59

78 A Louis XIV silver-gilt *écuelle* and cover made in Paris in 1672

79 Sweden has had many famous gold-smiths: a punch-bowl by Johan Jönsson Holm, Stockholm, *c.* 1715

of the century, is still marked, but these are made in decreasing numbers [figure 54]. A new development in about 1650 was the fashion for equestrian statuettes, some purely ornamental, others designed as wine-flasks.

As in the previous century, Germany produced some outstanding craftsmen, one of the greatest of whom was Johann Andreas Thelot of Augsburg. A prolific and exceptionally gifted worker, he signed a great deal of his work, although not always marking it. He made cups, dishes, tankards and many other pieces of domestic and ecclesiastical silver, but is most famous for his beautiful relief work. Johann Thelot (1654-1734) was of French origin, though his family had been settled in Germany for some generations, one of the many, no doubt, who over a period of centuries sought more stable working conditions abroad. The themes of his reliefs are religious, mythological, or of contemporary events, a favourite at this time being the defeat of the Turks at the gates of Vienna in 1683, the culminating victory of Sobieski over the Islamic forces. Overcrowded though his work may be, technically it is comparable with the finest Dutch reliefs and his fluidity and naturalistic figure modelling is quite outstanding. Perhaps the most competent goldsmith of the period in Augsburg, he was merely one of a flourishing and technically extremely competent school.

80 A Charles II casket with *Chinoiserie* engraving, London, 1683

81 A George I tea-kettle by Samuel Margas, 1715. These kettles often stood on a separate stand about 3 ft high

German taste has always been predominantly ornate and the simpler forms found running parallel with decorative silver in other countries at this time rarely occur. French influence did finally begin to dominate German design, and plain pieces were produced from about 1700, although it was still unusual to encounter an absolutely unadorned article [figure 74]. Cut-card work was not common and the French ornament which was so wholeheartedly adopted in England was adopted by the German goldsmith in his own individualistic way.

As in England and France, silver furniture was one of the extravagances of the age, and judging by the few surviving examples, the majority of these were made in Augsburg [figure 62]. Three pieces are in Sweden. As a European power after her success in the Thirty Years' War, her taste for luxury rapidly developed and it is most likely that with a relatively undeveloped goldsmiths' industry, the Swedish princes and nobility used to order from the Augsburg or Nuremberg guilds. At all events two superb chandeliers and the Swedish throne chair, all mid-seventeenth-century Augsburg work, have survived, and a table of slightly earlier date is at Rosenborg Castle in Copenhagen. As one would expect at this period, the style is flamboyant and rather ornate, one of the candelabra particularly showing the influence of the Dutch grotesque

82 A pair of George I octagonal wine-coolers by William Lukin, 1716. It is difficult to distinguish between French and English silver of this date.

mask technique. In Denmark a table top and a firescreen made by early eighteenth-century Augsburg goldsmiths have been preserved at Rosenborg Castle, Copenhagen, ornate by comparison with contemporary French and English work, with the Baroque influence still apparent. If there was comparable furniture from France and England to study, it would almost certainly have been in a plainer style, but in Germany simple forms rarely remained popular for long periods. The same applies to the suite of silver furniture belonging to the Dukes of Brunswick, of approximately the same date and once again of Augsburg manufacture. Also rather ornate, these pieces are beautifully executed and the figure modelling employed is very fine. The fact that the German goldsmith, imitated by his Scandinavian counterpart, continued to produce silver-covered furniture is interesting: in England and France it is doubtful whether much was made after about 1700, if we except pieces like kettle stands, chandeliers, small mirrors and sconces [figure 72]. The Augsburg goldsmith continued to make furniture of this kind until the middle of the century when the use of ormolu and the adoption of other techniques made silver unfashionable.

Goldsmiths' work in Sweden and Denmark at this time should perhaps be mentioned briefly. As in Germany it is cups, beakers and tankards that survive in the greatest numbers, the Scandinavian countries preserving a distinct and individualistic style. All had guilds of considerable antiquity with systems of dating similar to those we have noted elsewhere, and in Stockholm (particularly by 1700) an extremely competent school of goldsmiths existed, whose work, in its own unmistakable way, bears comparison with any other country, influencing the Baltic States and Russia in their turn [figure 79]. The influence of Scandinavian upon Scottish and East Anglian goldsmiths' work is quite considerable in certain periods also. Although confining ourselves to the main centres of the goldsmiths' craft it should not be forgotten that the smaller European countries at different periods produced work of a similar standard which could well be studied at greater length.

By 1700 French design was beginning to dominate European work to a really remarkable degree and in Germany we see the same use of the classical medallion, the chased strapwork decoration and even the adoption of French forms to some degree. The cups, beakers and tankards which have been in vogue in Germany for so

83 An Italian dish, width 6¼ ins, c. 1720

long do not dominate the scene; instead we find the toilet sets, tea sets, candlesticks, dishes, salvers, plates and other pieces of more generally usable domestic silver, pleasing in outline but rarely completely plain and unadorned [figures 67, 75]. What decoration we find is generally confined to that mentioned above, although profusely ornamented dishes and general decorative relief work still occurs. Not only the silver furniture but the majority of German domestic plate at this time comes from the Augsburg workshops, which seem to have

84 A Louis XIV covered sugar bowl and a pair of table candlesticks made in Paris in 1711 and 1714

85 A Louis XIV parcel-gilt covered beaker, Paris, 1706

achieved the prominent position formerly held by Nuremberg at the turn of the previous century.

Italian goldsmiths' work during the period tends to be somewhat undistinguished by comparison with other countries. The supremacy which Italy enjoyed in the sixteenth century, having passed in turn to Germany, Holland and France, left the native industry without the impetus to produce outstanding work. The rather heavy Baroque forms still found favour in the latter half of the seventeenth century [figure 83], but the turn of the century saw the introduction of extremely plain work indeed. In fact between 1700 and 1730 Italy, using simple fluted forms with moulded borders, produced plate as simple as

any to be found elsewhere on the Continent, and although design may not be as outstanding as in France, some very attractive examples from this period are in existence. The Medici in Florence had become weak and ineffectual: the Papal court equally did not wield the power and influence which it had once enjoyed: this lack of active patronage of the arts resulted in a far greater production of secular silver and less emphasis on the ecclesiastical. It also meant that the goldsmith did not enjoy the prestige and prosperity of previous decades. As elsewhere we find the more common domestic pieces in considerable quantity, candlesticks, inkstands, dishes, coffee pots and similar articles. Italy, like the rest of Europe, became widely influenced by French design.

The trends all over Europe thus tended to be similar, with the ornate foliate and figure decoration of the late seventeenth century and the lingering influence of the Baroque giving way to plain forms, embellished to a greater or lesser degree from country to country. German and Dutch influence on European design gave way to French, which remained dominant for about a hundred years, after which national forms again tended to re-assert themselves. The next century was to see a far greater general use of domestic silver and another swing of the pendulum to exuberant and ornate decoration.

86 An American two-handled cup and cover by Charles Le Roux, New York, c. 1720

87 In the eighteenth century, Royal godchildren and Speakers of the House of Commons were generally given silver engraved with the Royal coat of arms: a George I four piece silver-gilt tea service and tray by Philip Rollos Jr, 1721

Rococo and Classical Inspiration

88 A Louis XV salt cellar by Antoine-Sebastien Durand, Paris, 1757, bearing the arms of Louis Philippe, Duc d'Orléans

ONCE AGAIN, IN BOTH France and England, in effect the year 1730 brings us to the start of two new reigns, George II succeeding to the English throne in 1727, Louis XV attaining his majority in 1723. Neither event had the influence on design that the accession of Charles II and the personal rule of Louis XIV brought in their time: the goldsmiths' fine tradition of workmanship, by now so firmly established in both countries, continued its steady development. Certain factors contributed a further tremendous expansion in the volume of goldsmiths' work. The most important of these is the final emergence in Europe of that new phenomenon, the wealthy middle class, patronising the goldsmith and introducing a greatly increased demand for the more ordinary pieces of domestic silver. The nobility and gentry continued to furnish their houses with silver on a still more lavish scale, and the crowned heads of the continent almost without exception ordered from Paris or adopted French designs, so great a reputation had Paris work achieved by this date.

Although the cataclysmic effect of the French Revolution of 1789 caused the destruction yet again of the vast majority of the pieces which were made in such abundance, a period of French silver had at length been reached which can today still furnish a really representative number of products. The 1730's saw the emergence of an entirely new style, divorced from the forms which, although more profusely chased and decorated than at the turn of the century, remained basically simple in outline. This Rococo style, with flowing sweeping lines, asymmetrical and employing stylised shell motifs and *rocaille* ornament, is supremely well suited, when competently worked, to silver

89 An Italian parcel-gilt inkstand, Rome *c.* 1730

90 A George II oval soup tureen and cover, made in London in 1734 by Paul de Lamerie, one of the most famous English makers and a master of the Rococo technique

91 A Queen Anne coffee pot by William Fawdery, London, 1704; and a George I Bullet teapot, London, 1723. The latter is without any ornament and relies for its effect on its proportions

forms. J.A. Meissonier was perhaps the greatest designer at this time although his practical experience appears to have been small, closely followed by Pierre Germain. The middle of the century is rich in competent craftsmen: of these the most famous are the Germain family, Thomas, his son François-Thomas and others [figures 95, 99, 112]. The middle of the eighteenth century was particularly notable for the remarkable orders for dinner services, which were considerable in their ramifications, involving as they did soup tureens, covers and stands, sauce tureens and boats, spice boxes, salts, cruets, casters, candlesticks and candelabra, soup and dinner plates, meat dishes, second-

92 A George I dessert dish by Paul de Lamerie, 1725. Lamerie's early work is comparatively plain

93 A German silver-gilt dish, 2 feet across, by Johann Erhard Henglin II, *c.* 1730

course dishes, chargers, knives, spoons and forks [figure 104]. The Germain family executed immense services for the Portuguese, the Russian and the French courts, of which a considerable number of pieces made for the two former have survived. When it is realised that the orders for the King of Portugal covered the years 1728 to 1766 it may be appreciated that the articles from this service alone will give a fair indication of the stylistic changes. The principal effect of the Rococo style was to give a fluidity, a sense almost of movement to a well designed piece of silver [figures 88, 100]. Many of the tureens, candelabra, condiment stands and other objects, despite the amazingly heavy gauge of metal in which they are constructed, have beautifully flowing lines, to which the addition of cast *rocaille* ornament, shells and foliage contribute. Finials realistically formed as vegetables, crustacea, animals and cherubs, accurately modelled, are common [figures 88, 104] Fine chasing, engraving and fluting complement this work. Stems of forks and spoons are cast and chased with foliate and other undulating designs and dishes and plates have shaped borders. The plain oblong or angular forms completely disappear, although even at the height of the Rococo period in the middle of the century the unornamented piece with perhaps simple moulding and guilloche borders may be encountered. Candlesticks and candelabra display a pleasing variety in design with crisply modelled husk, shell and foliate decoration. Apart from the dinner services which have been already well documented for many years, a fine example by Jacques Roettiers, another famous Court goldsmith, made in Paris between 1735 and 1738, recently came to light in England, where it had been in the possession of the Earls of Berkeley since it was first made [figure 104]. The existence of a goldsmithing industry where work was comparable to that in Paris made it most unusual for an Englishman to order French silver and this possibly unique example was made for the Berkeleys because of their association with that country. The third Earl's wife, Louise, was grand-daughter of the Duchesse d'Aubigny, a famous beauty and mistress of Charles II (from whom Louise was descended) and the Berkeleys were frequent visitors to Aubigny as a result: hence their order of this Paris service. This must, unfortunately for our study of French silver, be regarded as an isolated instance of such an order. It displays many of the fluid characteristics which we have noted, with

94 One of a pair of George II covered jugs, height 10½ ins, by Charles Kandier, 1733

95 A pair of Louis XV table candlesticks, height 9¾ ins, by Thomas Germain, a member of the famous family of French silversmiths, Paris, 1734

vegetable finials to the tureens, but it is really an example of the transitional period before the high Rococo was established. One interesting development, though not as marked in France as in England, is the introduction of a modicum of Chinese figure decoration, a feature of the mid-eighteenth-century passion for things Chinese [figure 109]. One does encounter, too, the rams' masks and festoon ornament very occasionally in the 1750's, some twenty years before it generally appears in England, but as usual French design was some two decades ahead. Meanwhile, with the domestic plate of all kinds which we take for granted today, the traditional French *écuelle*, the beaker and the little wine taster (which has not previously been mentioned) continue to be made in quantities, the two former more profusely decorated but essentially the same in outline.

Meanwhile, similar trends and demands for goldsmiths' work occurred in England. The London maker did not have the advantage of his Paris equivalent in being the enviable leader of European styles and techniques and therefore the recipient of large orders from foreign royalty and nobility, but he produced a remarkably large quantity of domestic silver of all kinds at this time, a very considerable proportion of which has happily survived. After 1730 (with very few exceptions) it is possible stylistically to recognise English silver at a glance: the Huguenot school, which still had a dominant influence, were mainly a generation born in the country and had developed a technique. which, though in origin French, showed strong native design. As we have noted, at most periods a decade or two behind France, style in England remains preponderantly plain until 1730 or a little later, relieved by applied forms of attractive cut-card work and strapwork with the use on occasion of medallions in the French style of fifteen or twenty years before, by degrees becoming more flowing and less formal. Engraving still continues to be quite outstanding, surpassing the French. By slow degrees the simplicity of form is abandoned, chasing and engraving become more profuse and less well defined and the use of similar decoration to that employed in France becomes fashionable, the *rocaille* ornament, the shells, flowers, crustacea, dolphins, *putti*, vine tendrils and other decorative features, much of which however is not duplicated abroad. This work too is carried out in a very heavy gauge of metal, a great deal of cast and chased work being usual

96 A German silver-gilt cup and cover made by Jacob Baur in Augsburg, 1735

at this time. Pieces which do not occur in France where coffee and chocolate are the common beverages, are the teapots, tea-kettles, caddies and the little milk jugs, the caddies very frequently appearing in wood or shagreen-cased sets of three [figures 98, 109]. The latter, together with tea-kettles, were favourite subjects of the Chinese decoration which was far more widely employed than in France. All the pieces of silver which today appear in profusion are made, casters, candlesticks and candelabra, epergnes, salvers, plate for the dinner table, large covered cups, mugs and tankards (almost always plain), and many other articles. It cannot be gainsaid on a direct comparison of the two that the English craftsman's interpretation of the Rococo style lacked the delicacy and refinement of the Frenchman's. Much of this silver is beyond criticism, but a proportion, either from heaviness in design or a somewhat exuberant use of decorative detail, fails to please in some respect. Technically it cannot be criticized; it is in the carrying out of his design, superbly executed though it may be, that the London goldsmith sometimes fails. Again it is among the Anglo-French names that we find the most extravagant employment of Rococo forms. Nicholas Sprimont's work [figure 106] for instance is noticeable for his employment of crustacea, lobsters and other denizens of the sea, not a common feature of English goldsmiths' products as a general rule. Another great master of the Rococo technique was Paul de Lamerie. It is interesting to note briefly the details of Lamerie's career as it illustrates the progress and success of a family of French Huguenot descent in England. He was born in 1688 in Holland where his father had been serving in the army of William of Orange, having left France before the revocation of the Edict of Nantes, and his family are first mentioned in London in 1691. The father appears subsequently in the Civil List as receiving a small Crown pension, from which it is obvious that those refugees who were unable to make a living (Lamerie's father was a gentleman born and an officer) received some help from the Crown. The son was apprenticed in 1703 for seven years to another Huguenot goldsmith, Pierre Platel, who was naturalised in 1679. Without exception, Platel's work is outstanding and Lamerie could not have chosen a more competent master. The latter became a master goldsmith in 1712 and from this time a steady flow of fine pieces from his hand are to be found, beginning with the simpler forms

97 A George II
silver-gilt side-board
ewer made by Paul
de Lamerie in 1736

98 A George II caddy set by Paul de Lamerie, London, 1735, in its contemporary case

[figure 92] relieved perhaps by fine flat-chasing, engraving or applied strapwork, masks and scrolls reminiscent of the French (designs imbibed no doubt from Platel) and becoming in the late seventeen-twenties steadily more ornate with much use of decorative cast and chased work, of which the ewer and basin made for the Goldsmiths' Company in 1741 are superb examples [figures 90, 97, 101]. Lamerie first became a Warden of the Company in 1743 and had he lived long enough would undoubtedly have become Prime Warden, but he died in 1751 before attaining this, the highest office a goldsmith could aspire to. He was at the time working in the height of the prevailing fashion with its richly extravagant decoration, and

99 A Louis XV oval sauceboat by Thomas Germain, 1738

100 This trefoil-shaped spice box belongs to the Berkeley dinner-service made by Jacques Roettiers. The cover revolves to reveal the interior of the boxes

even he, the master goldsmith, produces some plate which is either over-ornamented or ill-balanced in some respect. In general however his technique and finish are in a class of their own, and his influence on contemporary work must have been considerable [figures 98, 102]. Judging by the quantity of his pieces to have survived he obviously had a large workshop and besides numerous apprentices a number of workmen as well.

An Act in force between 1719 and 1757, which imposed a duty of sixpence per ounce on all silver at the time of assay, caused a number of goldsmiths to evade this tax, a heavy one for those days. One way in which this was done was to submit a small piece of a few ounces in weight for assay and marking, the marks being then cut out and applied to the base of a heavier object. At the same time, hall-marks of old silver from the last four decades of the seventeenth century, sent in probably to be refashioned, were cut out and applied in the same way, the new maker striking his mark over the former maker's mark and frequently defacing the date-letter. Pieces can be found with the maker's mark struck clearly once and deliberately indistinctly three other times in a crude attempt to depict a full set of four hall-marks. Legally these are unsaleable in England today, although they may be perfectly genuine and beautiful examples of the period, probably of the correct silver standard. An example of Lamerie's 'duty-dodging' is known. This practice ceased with the repeal of the Duty Act in this form and the introduction of the death penalty in 1757 for forging or transposing marks.

In some aspects the English goldsmith lacks the originality displayed by his French counterpart, apart from his somewhat heavier treatment of designs. An example of this lack of originality can be seen in candlesticks of the period. As they were no doubt made in the same profusion in France as in England it is remarkable how few French examples have survived, but those that do display a far greater variety of design than the English [figure 95]. John and William Cafe must have produced thousands of pairs of cast candlesticks in London during the course of their careers, but they tend to be of one stereotyped model with little imaginative decorative detail, compared with the crisp foliate, husk, shell and floral decoration with a multitude of border designs used in France. It is, however, perhaps a little invidious to compare the work of the two

101 A George II silver-gilt ewer and dish by Paul de Lamerie, 1741; part of the ceremonial plate of the Worshipful Company of Goldsmiths

countries, when comparisons are after all largely a matter of taste.

German work during this period of some forty years is a rather curious conglomeration of styles. Although large quantities of Augsburg and Nuremberg silver can still be found, the fact that even some of the Bavarian princes ordered their services and other domestic silver in France must have had an effect on the prosperity of the guilds there. In Vienna, too, one finds the emergence of a competent school of goldsmiths working largely to French designs, and in fact late in the century Vienna-made dinner services seem to outnumber German. The pieces of German silver which are most abundant at this time are still tankards, cups and beakers, the latter becoming more French in outline, the tankards and cups *repoussé* and chased with figure subjects or foliage; the beakers more often merely chased or engraved. A considerable number of toilet services were made too in the earlier half of the century. With the development of Rococo taste, which became particularly popular in South Germany, the use of *rocaille* work and shell motifs is predominant, just as it is in contemporary architecture. Floral designs, leafage and figures are also used and fluted decoration remains in vogue. Curiously at this time one does encounter a number of plain pieces side by side with the

102 A George II silver-gilt ewer and dish by Paul de Lamerie, 1736–7

decorative plate. French patterns for dishes, tureens, bowls and other articles are adopted: one even finds in Germany bowls and covers of *écuelle* type. The interpretation of the Rococo is perhaps a little ponderous, but some pleasing forms are developed, candlesticks and candelabra particularly achieving some flowing designs. One noticeable difference in German silver is the gauge: much of it tends to be lighter in the middle decades of the century than either English or French. In general German in-

103 A pair of Italian table candle-sticks made in Padua, *c.* 1740

104 One of the few surviving French services of this date: the Berkeley dinner service by Jacques Roettiers, Paris, 1735–1738, engraved with the contemporary arms of Augustus, fourth Earl of Berkeley

terpretation of French Rococo design is not altogether happy: the goldsmith often interpreted its forms rather crudely and with excessive, not very well-finished, elaboration of detail. Because of the Hanoverian connection with England, some North German goldsmiths'. work displays marked English characteristics, a rare example of English influence on German design, and quite brief. candlesticks, tureens, jugs, bowls and other domestic pieces retain basically their former outline. The Auguste

family in Paris became dominant in design and again completed large orders for foreign courts. The chief difference is in the decorative motifs which are used, the flower and laurel leaf festoons pendent from ribbon-ties,

105 A Louis XV chocolate pot, Paris, 1739

106 A George II silver-gilt centrepiece, probably by Nicholas Sprimont, London, 1741; in the possession of H. M. Queen Elizabeth II at Buckingham Palace

rings or rams' masks, the wide use of shallow flutes, the
re-appearance of acanthus and other formal leafage mostly
in *repoussé* or engraved work, while mustard pots, baskets
and cruet stands of predominantly open-work design with

107 The 'Cadaval' toilet set made in Paris in 1738 by Etienne Pollet, Antoine Lebrun, Sebastien Igonet and Alexis Loire III

glass liners begin to appear. Forms became rather less massive, lighter classical lines became more evident although the transition is gradual until the actual time of the Revolution. It can be assumed that, for a period of a year or two, while the heads were tumbling and the traditional patrons of the craft vanished overnight, the goldsmiths' trade was in a state of suspended animation. To the Revolution may be ascribed the loss of the vast majority of eighteenth-century pieces of French domestic silver, though this is partly attributable to another melting campaign carried through in 1759 to raise funds. There is no doubt that those who saw the approaching storm and left before it broke would have taken their personal plate with them as cash in hand and, penurious as many of them must have become, have melted it to raise funds. What remained in the country would have been looted or

108 A Louis XV *écuelle* and cover by Eloi Guérin, Paris, 1749

109 A set of Rococo tea caddies made in England, *c.* 1740

confiscated and suffered the same fate. We must be thankful that anything survived the wreck at all. At all events, when the trade began to recover in the 1790's an essentially new phase in design had begun, employing pseudo-classical motifs with decorative additions from time to time. The chief exponents of this style were Robert-Joseph and Henry Auguste, Biennais and Odiot, examples of whose work survive in profusion [figures 117, 120], Biennais, as Napoleon's goldsmith, being one of the more prolific makers [figure 123].

Italian goldsmiths' work during the Rococo period, unlike German, does not show any strong French influence until nearly the last quarter of the eighteenth century. As we have already seen in the earlier part of the century their work remains preponderantly plain, and this tendency continues, except for a few isolated examples of extremely competent cast and chased work with beautiful figure modelling, shells, leafage and scrolls, very much Baroque in taste, by such masters as Gagliardi. Where one would expect a rich use of Rococo ornament it is a little surprising to find the shell and floral motifs and *rocaille* work used with considerable restraint, whilst engraving, though

110 A pair of Italian silver-gilt table candlesticks, Turin, c. 1780

competently executed, is not outstanding. Candlesticks, coffee pots, dishes and many other pieces are frequently encountered with a minimum of decoration [figure 103], and it is quite obvious that the more extreme Rococo fashions never found much favour with the Rome goldsmith, who remained in this instance conservative, though achieving some most attractive baluster and vase-shaped forms, with moulded and waved borders to salvers, trays and similar pieces. Turin, as well as Rome in this century, produced a large amount of domestic plate [figure 110].

In France the somewhat hybrid designs which existed side by side were a result of the reluctance or inability of certain goldsmiths to adopt the Rococo styles. This led to profusely decorated and relatively plain silver being produced at the same time, and occasionally to combinations of the two. In either event this gave way between 1760 and 1770 to a new fashion derived from the classical, which again swept Europe and lasted in some form or another until the end of our period. This classical style became predominant by 1775, although in France, as we have noted, certain decorative features like the rams' masks and festooned ornament occurred even twenty years earlier. In the fifteen years prior to the Revolution in 1789 actual form did not change drastically: ewers and dishes,

111 A tea service by Paul Revere of Boston (1735–1815), made in 1799 for Edmund Hartt, at whose wharf the famous frigate *Constitution* had been built two years earlier

112 (*above*) A Louis XV coffee-pot by François-Thomas Germain, Paris, 1757. It is decorated with coffee leaves and berries

113 (*right*) An Italian covered jug made in Naples, *c*. 1740

A large quantity of the silver made during the Napoleonic period was gilt. Hitherto nothing has been said about the actual process of gilding which was extensively employed, particularly in the sixteenth century and earlier. Gilding by the old method was accomplished by a process known as fire-gilding, which was not replaced by electro-gilding until about one hundred years ago. The pieces in its completed state was thoroughly cleaned, after which an amalgam of gold and quicksilver was made and spread evenly over the object to be gilt. The surface

114 An inkstand made in Padua, c. 1760

115 A pair of Louis XV table candlesticks by Edmé-Pierre Balzac, Paris, 1767

was then heated, the quicksilver evaporated and the gold fused as a thin layer to the surface of the silver. Like most of the old methods, fire-gilding produces a piece of better colour with more resistance to wear, but the fumes produced are injurious to health and consequently it is an illegal process, at least in England today. Electro-gilding is neither so resistant to wear nor does it produce so pleasing a colour.

As a style the neo-classical becomes far more universal in France than any previous form, and as before, French designs have considerable influence abroad, although not in England at this period, where a native version of the classical form was being developed. In Germany and Italy French designs were imitated although again applied with some individuality. Jugs, ewers and coffee pots become oviform, and narrow necked, either fitted with traditional wood handles or replaced by classical figures. Bowls, dishes and tureens become shallower and of plain circular or oval outline [figure 120]. Cups take on a plain bell shape, vases of classical outline appear, candlesticks tend to take a tapered baluster form. Decorative features are generally cast, chased and applied with extreme precision. This takes the form of anthemion and honeysuckle, acanthus, tightly scrolled flower heads and other formal designs with borders of flowers, beads or leafage, generally stamped. Feet are made as winged sphinxes, griffins or swans and decoration of an Egyptian flavour, inspired no doubt by Napoleon's campaigns in that country, remained popular for some years, as did female figures, gods and goddesses, *putti* and mythological creatures. Handles, apart from the looped wooden handle general in vessels holding hot liquids, take the form of winged female figures, children, Medusa heads, snakes and other classical forms. Until Napoleon's defeat the imperial eagle as a finial is a popular feature. Applied, cast and chased work is almost universal at this date and the amount of engraving carried out is small. Although one may criticise the machine-like precision at this time, the finish is quite brilliant, and an almost jewel-like crispness is achieved. This is not perhaps the happiest of designs to translate into silver, being of purely architectural inspiration and of necessity limiting the maker in his efforts to achieve the flowing line which is one of the beauties of goldsmiths' work, but these pieces, particularly after 1810 when much of the decorative work is dropped and the forms are retained, are at least of

116 An Italian coffee-pot, Lucca, *c.* 1770

117 An Empire silver-gilt tea and coffee service by Jean-Baptiste-Claude Odiot, Paris, *c.* 1810

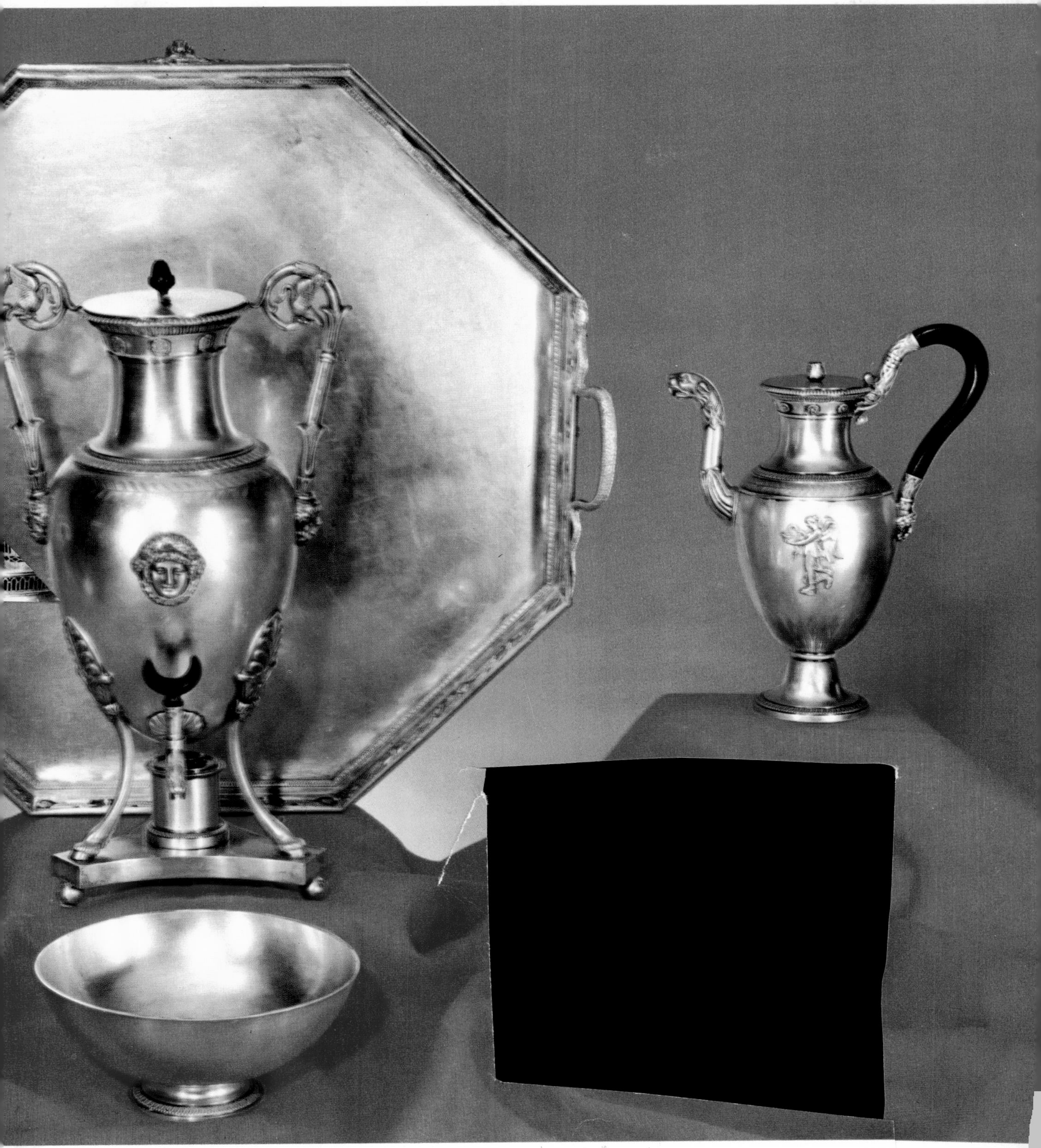

considerable elegance, which is more than can be said of English work at the same time. Plainer forms, relieved only by stamped borders, date approximately from the restoration of the monarchy in France in 1815 and continue well into the middle of the century.

In Italy, naturally, the re-emergence of classical form and design was seized upon with much more enthusiasm by the goldsmiths of Rome. In the period up to about 1800 one tends to find rather more ponderous silver than in France though with similar decorative influences, the foliate festoons, the scroll and beaded borders, the feet headed by animal or human masks and the figure finials. This appears on most of the widely used domestic plate in some form or another, but again in rather more restrained designs [figure 116], based on native classical rather than pseudo-classical forms, nor is the decoration as crisp or sharp as the French. Though similar designs for coffee pots, tureens, bowls and other pieces are introduced, the intricate cast and chased decoration which is such a feature of French Empire goldsmiths' work is not practised in Italy; half lobing or chased leafage are far more common with perhaps a foliate band, beaded or key pattern borders, bird or figure finials, the handles being, in common with the French, formed as snakes, heads, scrolls and other types similar to those already described. Spouts are more often formed as demi-figures, melusines and similar creatures or merely terminating in a grotesque animal mask, and the oil lamps with projecting fonts which are so typically Italian and date from the eighteenth century have figure or columnar formed stems, the latter often _____ bust. Although Italian work in this classical _____ ot have the finish of its French counterpart, _____ es not suffer from a surfeit of minute detailed _____ d in its own individual way is a pleasing _____ of the style inspired by the French.

_____ ork was rather less affected by the pseudo- _____ s. In outline her silver at least remained _____ c, the narrow necked coffee pots and jugs _____ neral in Italy and France rarely occurred. _____ forms of teapot and coffee pot tended to _____ cylindrical and oval types, engraved or _____ ten rather crudely, with festoons and some- times applied with medallions. Handles, feet and finials remained quite simple and a certain amount of pierced work in mustard pots, salt cellars, and small baskets is

118 An Itali

119 This soup tureen cover and stand by Jacques Roettiers, Paris, 1770, was one of twenty-two tureens and stands ordered by Catherine the Great of Russia for Prince Orloff

found. The most popular form of border ornament is the bead. After the turn of the century silver of a lighter gauge is generally used and what little classical influence there is disappears. Silver design becomes a little nondescript and in due course, as it does in England, degenerates into a rather tasteless over-ornamented style.

Returning finally to England, for the first time in her long goldsmithing history we can genuinely point to a truly native style, classically inspired though it may be. The decorative motifs which we noted in French silver in the 1750's are not found in England until twenty years have elapsed, but at the start of George III's reign in 1760 classically-lobed and fluted column candlesticks with

Corinthian capitals do begin to appear, side by side with the more ornate Rococo forms and the *Chinoiserie* decoration which persists for some five years. Before describing the essential differences in English goldsmiths' work it is necessary briefly to mention the commencement at this period of the manufacture of Sheffield plate, that is plate made by fusing thin silver sheets on to a copper ingot, rolling it and then making domestic articles by techniques similar to the goldsmiths'. This 'fused plate' process rapidly developed into a very large business, both in Sheffield and Birmingham, with the use for the first time of die-stamping, machine piercing and other mass manufacturing processes. This had several effects upon the London goldsmiths: similar techniques were adopted in silver and to compete with the cheaper Sheffield plate article a tendency to use a lighter gauge of silver arose. This latter factor was partly due to contemporary design, but it must also have been forced upon the goldsmith by the need to compete economically with the extremely successful plate, which created a new market.

The development of the classical style in London was rapid and for the first time an English architect is responsible for original designs in goldsmiths' work. Robert Adam, supremely successful as an architect, meticulously designed not only the houses which he was commissioned to build, but the contents, the furniture, carpets and silver, and much of this has survived. Adam's designs are graceful; not all contemporary English work can be said to be [figure 122]. As in France and Italy the ram's mask and festoon decoration becomes very popular, particularly between 1770 and 1780, and the husk, laurel or drapery festoon with beaded and formal foliate borders very typical. Silver in a lighter gauge becomes more common: candlesticks tend to be either light castings or die-stamped and then filled with pitch to add body, with weighted bases. The heavy cast forms virtually disappear. Pierced work, very light indeed, is found in sweetmeat baskets, salt cellars and cake baskets; casters are also often of too light a gauge and sometimes ill-balanced. Boat-shaped forms for tureens and salt cellars become popular [figure 124]. These are generally completely unadorned after about 1780 except perhaps for an engraved coat of arms or decorated with bright-cut engraving which is such an attractive development for about fifteen years between 1796 and 1810, with simple reeded, beaded or lightly

120 An Empire silver-gilt soup tureen and cover by Jean-Baptiste-Claude Odiot, Paris, c. 1810, showing the sphinxes made fashionable by Napoleon's Egyptian campaign

engraved borders. The twenty years between 1780 and 1800 are productive of some of the most graceful plain silver to be found, excepting only the early years of the century.

This eclipse of classical design was only temporary: as we have seen, the fashion continued unbroken in France. Many contemporary critics did not care for Adam's designs: George III himself voiced the opinion that they were too neat and pretty. Another English designer, Charles Tatham, published in 1806 fresh designs condemning 'light and insignificant forms' and championing heavier patterns, both in weight of metal and conception. Even before these were published the trend was for heavier, more ornamental, plate to be used, and although design was quite different, there is more affinity with French work during this time. The winged sphinx Egyptian motif occurs as does cast and chased work in low relief, classical figures, formal leafage in acanthus, laurel, anthemion, palmette and other forms, with snake, mask or scroll handles. Another form of ornament not generally

121 A Louis XVI ewer and basin by Joseph-Theodore Vancoubert, Paris, 1781

encountered in France is the wide use of vineleaves, bunches of grapes and Bacchanalian figures and scenes. Technically, as in Paris, the work on all these decorative motifs is exceptionally good, crisp and clear, although in some cases the richness of ornamental detail gives one a foretaste of the over-profuse decoration encountered shortly afterwards. By 1820 Tatham's strictures about light forms has been amply vindicated: the gauge of silver employed was as heavy as it had ever been and decorative detail unfortunately was becoming steadily more so too. Engraving at this time was virtually confined to inscriptions and armorials, and cannot be said to be comparable with that of earlier periods. Indeed from this time the art of engraving all over Europe begins to decline.

One maker during the early nineteenth century is outstanding in London, Paul Storr, although others, notably Benjamin Smith, were equally competent craftsmen. One interesting aspect of Storr's career is his patronage by the Prince Regent, later George IV. As the only one of the Hanoverian Kings to be interested in the arts, George IV was unfortunately instrumental in sending the bulk of the Royal plate in 1817 and finally in 1823 to

122 Robert Adam's designs had considerable influence on English silver: a pair of George III three-light candelabra by John Carter, 1774, designed by Robert Adam

be refashioned in the current taste, yet a further illustration of the hazards to which goldsmiths' work was exposed, even in a country free from revolution and invasion, showing that as recently as the early nineteenth century it was unheard of to preserve a piece on account of its age. As a result, a large quantity of the Royal silver is from the hand of Storr, much of it in his most massive and grandiloquent style. After 1830 even his work has the stamp of mass production about it and large ornate centrepieces, and other pieces of plate, well finished but of no aesthetic interest whatsoever, bear his mark. By contrast with the plain French silver of the 1820's the English product becomes increasingly more profusely decorated until outline disappears under a welter of tasteless decoration a decade later.

What conclusions can one reach today from this necessarily superficial survey of four countries covering three and a quarter centuries, a potentially limitless subject? It is obvious that silver design in the past has always been the result of some creative impulse inspired first by one country and then by another, stemming basically in very many instances from the Greco-Roman classical

123 An Empire silver-gilt supper set by Martin-Guillaume Biennais, Paris, c. 1810. Biennais was the fashionable goldsmith of his day

124 Two of a set of George III sauce tureens and covers, London, 1785, and one of a pair of George III cups and covers, Sheffield, 1801. These pieces are all in the classical manner

traditions, applied, interpreted and developed in a great variety of ways. The nineteenth century has seen the submergence of these distinctive styles in flamboyant and largely ill-conceived decorative detail, and the early twentieth century has tended to be a period of reproduction of earlier forms. No well defined European national style has been produced today with sufficient impact on designers and makers to cause the development of distinctive new fashions, but in common with the other arts it must be only a question of time before a fresh conception of goldsmiths' work is developed. Silver is unlikely ever to be bettered in its various widely used forms by the discovery of a more pleasing raw material and we must hope that some fresh, vigorous artistic trend, comparable to those which the goldsmith adapted with such conspicuous success in the past, will soon become apparent. As it is, we are left looking back at the distinctive styles of other centuries, the influence of the Renaissance and Baroque periods, the simplicity of the late seventeenth and early eighteenth centuries, the flowing Rococo designs and the neo-classical revival. Each period may have its admirers or detractors but all are complementary to each other; and the admirer or owner of a beautiful piece of silver, however small, has an integral part of the artistic and historical development of its country of origin at his fingertips.